Film

As a search for meaning

Ernest Ferlita and John R. May

Film
As a search for meaning

Veritas Publications Dublin 1977

This edition 1976 by
Veritas Publications,
Pranstown House, Booterstown Avenue, Co. Dublin.

First Published by Paulist Press, New York.

Cover by Steven Hope
Printed and bound in the Republic of Ireland
by Cahill (1976) Limited, Dublin.

ISBN 0–905092–31–7
Cat. No. 3349

In
memory
of our brother
ROY E. SCHILLING, S.J.
1928-1974

ACKNOWLEDGMENTS

Our research would have been extremely burdensome without the constant and generous assistance of Brother Alexis Gonzales, F.S.C., University Professor, Loyola University of New Orleans. We are also indebted to Mrs. Maria Landry and Maurice Bostick for their faithful work in typing the manuscript at different stages, and to the FBI (Film Buffs' Institute) of Loyola for processing the films for our Common Curriculum course "Film Journey," from which this work springs.

A Research Expense Grant from the Academic Grant Fund of Loyola University helped defray the cost of typing and duplicating the manuscript, and the editorial staff of the *New Orleans Review* kindly granted permission to reshape material that appeared as a Perspective in Vol. 2, No. 1, of that journal under the title "Care, Sorrow, and Troubled Joy: *Alice's Restaurant*."

Contents

Introduction

THE SEARCH FOR MEANING

Marshall McLuhan has made commonplace the cultural axiom that when one environment is replaced by another, the content of the old environment becomes nonfunctional and aesthetic. One culture uses a piece of pottery, the next places it in a museum. As with most generalizations, one is inclined here to demur, especially when applied to modes of communication. A superficial reflection on television's succession to the cultural primacy held earlier this century by cinema is no indication that cinema was not always—by those who understood it best—considered an art form or that today it is no longer functional.

Our affirmation about film would be simply this: It has always, at its best, been artistic in the fullest sense of the word and exercised a strong moral influence on its audience. Commenting on mere entertainment and critical appreciation as recognizable responses to cinema, Roy Huss and Norman Silverstein in *The Film Experience* insist that "even the earliest uses of moving pictures were not to entertain, but to put reality in a new light for the sake of better *perceiving* it."[1] The director of a film, of course, also *shapes* physical reality to his artistic vision; and it is precisely here that analysis becomes important, even indispensable, because of the subtle moral power exerted by the configured images of a film.

Cinema is attracting far fewer Americans than it did twenty-five years ago (less than twenty million a week now against seventy-five then), but its audience today is more clearly defined: It is younger and, generally, more sophisticated. And even if the desire to be entertained may still be a pervasive motive for going, entertainment is no longer the only goal, if indeed it ever was. Today's youth, products of high school and college film clubs and courses, go beyond mere experience to formal appreciation. Far more than previous generations, they use the language of film, of composition, movement, and editing. More viewers today are sensitive, above all, to the way a director shows and shapes reality to his own philosophical or religious viewpoint. Whether we care to accept it or not, cinema is this century's most original and compelling art form.

Now if one's aesthetic is truly and fully human, art is definitely viewed as related to life; traditionally, great art on one level at least has been considered an expression of man's hope a celebration of life's promise that transcends the individual to reach out to and sustain the aspirations of others. Cinema of all art forms, because of its unique representation of action in time and space, is ideally suited to the portrayal of the most basic of all human drives—the quest for meaning in one's personal life and for the meaning of existence as such.

Cinema is one of the most potent sources of contemporary insight into life's meaning (all too often a portrayal of its absence) precisely because of the vastness of its audience and the controlled effect of its images. In *Film Odyssey* we are concerned with analysis that leads to meaning. And we are interested in meaning wherever it is found, whatever its deepest roots in the artist's imagination. The creators of films, like their viewers, are both believers and nonbelievers. As analysts we speak consistently, we hope, from an appreciation of the universal language of film itself; our presuppositions concerning life's promise, however, are Judaeo-Christian in origin. That cinema is open to this tradition scarcely needs demonstration; that certain elements of the art of film are the parents and children of hope perhaps does.

When the astronaut in Stanley Kubrick's *2001: A Space Odyssey* plunges toward Jupiter, he continues a journey through time and space that began with the very rise of consciousness. "Where do I come from? What am I? Where am I going?" These are questions that surface in every age because the answers are never definitive. The depths of being are inexhaustible.

The search for meaning is implicit in every man's life. Man's life moves on two levels, one exterior, the other interior. A film like *2001: A Space Odyssey* imitates life on both these levels. The pull of Jupiter is also the pull of the future. Exteriorly, astronaut David Bowman goes on a mission that begins on earth and ends on one of Jupiter's moons. Interiorly, he moves yet deeper into the mystery of being. As dramatic action, the first level is a literal journey through time and space. It becomes, on the second level, a metaphor for the journey of the spirit. The first level is the level of plot; the second is the level of meaning. The first is the level of visual/aural reality; the second is the level of spiritual reality. They belong together like body and soul.

If man's meaning lies in the depths of being, the pull of the future is not merely the march of time. It is possible to move forward in time and yet stand still or fall back. The pull of the future is a call. From a biblical perspective, it is the call of God. God himself may be understood in terms of the future: "I will be who I will be." This is the answer that the Lord gives to Moses when Moses asks him his name, a more accurate translation of that expression in Exodus 3, 14 generally rendered as "I am who I am."[2] Like a pillar of fire. God goes before his people, calling them to be what they will be. The final image of *2001* of the Star Child revolving in space is resonant with that call.

Man, of course, can refuse to answer. Once the evolution of man's destiny is seen as a pilgrimage, it is not surprising to find man's sin described by biblical writers in related terms. To sin is to miss the road (*hata*) or to wander from it (*avon*). To repent is to return (*shuv*).[3] What we are asked to imagine is a man losing the right way and finding it again. The image has temporal as well as spatial dimensions. The man who stays on the road *hopes* in time to reach his destination. The man who *despairs* of ever reaching it feels time like a weight upon his back, and he sits down by the side of the road. The man who *presumes* to reach it on his own, breaks out of time, leaving the road for what seems to be a shortcut. Despair and presumption are two faces of man's original sin.

The hope that concerns us here is what certain writers refer to as fundamental hope.[4] It is the difference between "I hope" and "I hope that . . ." The latter has reference to all of the possibilities that this world can offer, to a specific value corresponding to a specific desire; whereas the former apparently has no such object. Gabriel Marcel almost seems to suggest that this fundamental hope has no object at all. Similarly, Ignatius Loyola in his *Spiritual Exercises* writes that God alone can give consolation to the soul without any previous cause, that is, "without any preceding awareness or knowledge of anything (*de algun objecto*) that could be said to have induced such consolation." Clearly it has to do, not with what a person *has*, but with what he *is*. Karl Rahner sees it as the experience of man's complete openness to God as his last end. This is not unlike Josef Pieper's tentative conclusion that fundamental hope has as its aim the salvation of the human person.

A further consideration may strike us at first as very strange. We may even wish to reserve judgment on it until we can verify it for ourselves in experience, and yet the experience is one that we would rather do without. It is this: "Fundamental hope" asserts itself most tellingly only when all our "hopes" collapse and lose their meaning. The experience is observed by a number of writers. Pieper finds it in controlled studies of people "for whom hope had become a problem in a unique way—the psychological situation of persons incurably ill, and of those who have attempted to take their own lives."[5] Viktor Frankl (whose testimony we shall later explore in greater detail) finds it in a Nazi death camp: "In a last violent protest against the hopelessness of imminent death, I sensed my spirit piercing through the enveloping gloom. I felt it transcend that hopeless, meaningless world, and from somewhere I heard a victorious 'Yes' in answer to my question of the existence of an ultimate purpose."[6] Erich Fromm finds it in what he calls the dynamic psalms, as in Psalm 22 ("My God, my God, why have you forsaken me?") where the movement "starts in some despair, changes to some hope, then returns to deeper despair and reacts with more hope; eventually it arrives at the very deepest despair and only at this point is the despair really overcome." He concludes with the seeming paradox that "despair can be overcome only if it has been fully experienced."[7] That paradox makes itself keenly felt in films like *Scarecrow* and *Nazarin*.

Hope, then, is man's relationship to his final meaning, to his beginning and end, to Someone or Something beyond himself that begins to answer the question of his being. Despair and presumption are his alienation from it. These two faces of man's original sin distort all his relationships—to himself, to his neighbor and world, to his God.

In this perspective, the search for meaning becomes a journey toward reconciliation. The personal dimension of that search addresses the issue of man's alienation from self; it impels him to a sense of his own worth. The social dimension responds to his alienation from neighbor and world; it urges him to form community. The religious dimension responds to his alienation from his beginning and end; it pulls him into the future, into the depths of God.

The search for meaning surely begins with the attempt to sense one's own worth. We are not born with that sense, and in this world of ours we never perfectly achieve it: We are always on the way, on a pilgrimage toward self-realization. That pilgrimage is marked by three essential experiences: (1) by trusting and mastering the world around us, (2) by being loved, and (3) by loving. The child very soon finds himself immersed in the world of things. "This is mine" are among the first words he learns to say, and before he knows it, "This is mine" means "This is me." If he forgets his list of what is his, he will not know who he is. By extending himself over his little empire, he begins to define himself in terms of it. Some people never outgrow this experience, or else, like Hester Grahame in *The Rocking-horse Winner*, they revert to it in their adult years when the experiences of being loved and loving are suppressed.

Ordinarily, these two experiences follow quickly upon the initial experience of trusting and mastering the world. A child begins to sense his own worth when the adult world, especially in the person of his mother, bends over him in affection. He knows he is lovable because he is loved. When love is withheld, as in *East of Eden*, the road to self-acceptance is painful indeed. From the very beginning the child needs the other in order to become himself. He becomes himself in the other's presence. And as he matures, and learns to reciprocate love, he will tell others that they are lovable by loving them; they will become themselves in *his* presence. The danger comes in attempting to *define* oneself in terms of the other. Part of the difficulty in the forming of community in *Alice's Restaurant* is to be found here. The process of becoming a person is a process of involvement and detachment, of solitude and society, of embrace and release.

Our relationship to ourselves, then, presupposes our relationship to others, a spiraling outward into a world of ever-increasing complexity, a world that both invites and threatens, a world of communion in which we can be at home with ourselves and yet not be alone. "Only communion," Robert Johann remarks, "at once preserves the miracle of originality that is the person, while at the same time healing the isolation that became his lot when self-consciousness first wrenched him from the mothering embrace of nature."[8] The family, the neighborhood, the city, the nation, the world—these are the structures for community, and yet each one can become a prison. Do they free us or hinder us in our search for meaning? Do they help us create our future, as the old America of *Easy Rider* was supposed to have done, or do they render us, in effect, futureless, as the town of Anarene in *The Last Picture Show* leaves its inhabitants?

A man asking these questions a century ago would not have had to reckon with one important element that we must reckon with today. And that element is technology. There is no disputing that technology puts into the hands of man a power to create new forms of freedom, new images of the future—so long as it remains technology. What happens when technology becomes technologism, that is, when it ceases to be a tool and becomes instead a "savior"? When that happens, instead of liberating man, it envelops, conditions, and determines him. Man no longer simply uses technology; he becomes a part of the total technological system. Consequently, he becomes one-dimensional, as Herbert Marcuse describes him, "incapable of critical thinking and action, futureless and ahistorical, at home in a system that is now his home and his permanent tomorrow."[9]

And what if the system is threatened? Since it is the embodiment of all that is good, a god unto itself, it must preserve itself at all costs. It engages in that abuse of technology called modern warfare. It perpetrates and suffers the irrationalities of a *Slaughterhouse-Five*.

The religious dimension pushes the personal and the social as far as they can go and then comes into its own. If the experience of being loved assures us that we are of value, the love of God not only assures us, but actually creates that value. God's love makes us be and be of value. If we are impelled into communion with others, our relationship to God not only provides the ground of our dignity as human beings but becomes the very basis of fellowship. God stands in the same mutual relationship to every member of the community.

Man experiences his relationship to God as Father, Word, and Spirit. It is possible, according to Gregory Baum, to translate the reality of God's trinitarian life into declarations about human life and to show that man's belief in God is the way to self-awareness.[10] "God is love," says St. John, and man experiences that love as beginning and end, as origin and destiny (Father). "To believe that God is Father is to become aware of oneself not as stranger . . . but as son."[11] In *Nazarin* we have the contradiction of a dedicated person trying to enter the mystery of love without loving.

If God is man's destiny, man will also experience God as call (Word), a call to lose one's self in order to find it. "To believe that God is Word is to become aware of oneself . . . as listener, as open-ended, as essentially unfinished, as still in the process of coming to be."[12] The anguish of Andreas in *The Passion of Anna* is that he has locked himself in silence. But the reality of God not only addresses man as origin and destiny (Father) and calls to him to pass beyond himself (Word) but unfolds in the center of his being as a source of creativity and new life (Spirit). To believe that God is Spirit is to become aware of oneself "as open to the radically new that emerges out of one's inner life yet forever transcends one's own resources."[13] When all the fonts of life are poisoned we find ourselves in the world of *Fellini Satyricon*.

Ultimately, the question is not so much, Is there a God? but rather (as for Antonius Block in *The Seventh Seal*), Is there a God to hope in? Is there a deathless source of power and meaning that will "reach from end to end mightily and order all things sweetly?" For Sam Keen, the question of God can be posed in no other way:

> To deny that there is a God is functionally equivalent
> to denying that there is any ground for hope. It is
> therefore wholly consistent for Sartre to say that
> human beings "must act without hope," or for Camus
> to warn that hope was the last of the curses which
> Pandora took from her box. If God is dead, then
> death is indeed God, and perhaps the best motto for
> human life is what Dante once wrote over the entrance
> to hell: "Abandon hope, all ye who enter."[14]

If there is any ultimacy to the meaning man searches for, only
God can provide it.

One of the most compelling contemporary tributes to
man's quest for meaning is undoubtedly the testimony of Viktor
Frankl in his account of the challenge of survival at Auschwitz
and other Nazi prisons. His *Man's Search for Meaning* (originally *From Death-Camp to Existentialism*) is the journal of a
man who discovered the will to live despite the oppressive fact
that the concentration camps had stripped him of every possession, material and spiritual, save naked existence. After three
years in bestial conditions he emerged from the horror of imminent death to learn that his wife, mother and father, and brother
had all perished in the camps; a sister alone survived the nightmare of genocide. What he discovered during those years he
expresses in Nietzsche's words: "He who has a *why* to live can
bear with almost any *how*."

Frankl's theory of existential analysis is hailed as one of
the most significant recent contributions to psychiatry. Logotherapy (the Greek word *Logos* means "word," denotes "meaning") is quite different from Freudian psychoanalysis. If the patient in psychoanalysis must lie on a couch (Frankl quotes an
American doctor as quipping) and *tell* the analyst things that
may be very unpleasant to reveal, logotherapy would have him
remain sitting erect and *hear* things that may be very disagree-
able to hear. Psychoanalysis deals with the patient's past, logotherapy with his future. Frankl proclaims man's will to meaning against Freud's will to pleasure and Adler's will to power.
The task of man as of the patient in logotherapy is to discover
the meaning that life holds out for him in the future. Thus
Frankl delimits his theory from another major influence on the

modern mind, Jean-Paul Sartre's insistence that man invents his meaning or "essence." John Barth in his sardonic little novel *The End of the Road* has provided in the Doctor a brilliant caricature of the hazards of thinking that man is perfectly free to determine the role that he will play in life. The title, preserved in Aram Avakian's film adaptation, shows clearly how man's imagination gravitates toward the imagery of journey for his statements of meaning, even if only to indicate a cul-de-sac.

If man detects meaning or *is pulled* by life's values, it is clear that there must be a radical freedom involved in man's quest. Happily for us, Frankl speaks for a vision of man who is free to choose from the meanings that life offers, thus rejecting the atmosphere of determinism that has pervaded so many of the twentieth-century portraits of man since Freud. "Ultimately, man should not ask what the meaning of his life is," Frankl writes, "but rather must recognize that it is *he* who is asked. In a word, each man is questioned by life; and he can only answer to life by *answering for* his own life; to life he can only respond by being responsible."[15] The purpose of human existence therefore is to transcend self, not simply to actualize the self. Frankl insists that self-actualization as such is an impossible goal; it can be expected only as a by-product of self-transcendence.

Frankl's analysis of the ways in which man discovers meaning is close to being the kind of specific tool that aids the cultural critic in discerning the depth of meaning in contemporary trends. According to Frankl, we can discover meaning in life in three different ways: (1) by the achievement or accomplishment of a deed, (2) by experiencing some*thing*, such as nature and art, or by experiencing some*one*, i.e., through love, and finally (3) by suffering. The meaning derived from achievement and through the experience of values and persons requires little or no explanation in comparison with what Frankl calls "the deepest meaning, the meaning of suffering."[16] This is meaning that one can discover only at that formidable, inescapable moment when one faces a fate that cannot be changed, such as an incurable disease or the death of a loved one. Man's main concern, Frankl argues, is neither pleasure nor the avoidance of pain, but rather to find meaning in his life; hence he is even ready to suffer provided that suffering has a meaning.

"Suffering ceases to be suffering in some way," he writes, "at the moment it finds a meaning, such as the meaning of a sacrifice."[17]

Although qualifications may have to be made and the question of emphasis resolved, Akira Kurosawa's *Ikiru* shows man's discovery of meaning on each of these levels. Mr. Watanabe, forced by the imminence of death to confront the mystery of existence, realizes through suffering that he has no life to save so he sacrifices his remaining days to the single-handed direction of a previously blocked civic project—the construction of a playground—that is ultimately best understood as a work of love for young children. Frankl clearly treats the *individual's* search for meaning inasmuch as the logotherapist deals with a single person, yet there is decidedly a sense in which his ways of discovering meaning apply to the social and religious dimensions of meaning as well as to the personal, as we have defined them. Each of the films that we analyze in this volume reveals a director's sensibility to the visual dimensions of journey that repeatedly confirm Frankl's principal sources of spiritual meaning.

* * *

Film Odyssey is the fruit of our experience with an undergraduate course entitled "Film Journey." Loyola University's recently reorganized Common Curriculum offers two types of courses, Dialogue Courses and Mode-of-Thought Courses. "Film Journey" is of the former variety, courses that challenge students to respond to the perennial and innovative values of man. The Dialogue Course is a modification of the Great Books format. Each week there is a substantial text to be read or, as in the case of "Film Journey," a film to be viewed. Since the course is team-taught, we alternate in giving the lectures that prepare the students for the screenings. Our analyses of films in Parts I-III of this work result from lectures prepared over the past four years. The films are scheduled, if possible, according to the deepening pattern of meaning—personal, social, and religious. Each week's screening is followed by small group discussions for which the students are regularly required to prepare and submit a one-page "position paper," modeled on the letter to the editor. They are expected to agree or disagree—reasonably—with whatever it is they understand the director's viewpoint concerning life's possibilities to be. These written responses, a stimulus for discussion, involve both interpretation and evaluation.

With minor exceptions, dictated mostly by a desire for orderly presentation, the divisions of our work correspond to the major emphases of the course. The body of screenings (nine or ten in a normal semester) is preceded by three or four introductory lectures intended to open up the dimensions of meaning in human existence. The substance of these lectures is offered here in our Introduction; the footnotes represent valuable source material for extended treatment of the theology of hope and its fundamental human expression as quest for meaning. A final introductory lecture is devoted to a definition of the principal elements of film technique, especially those related to quest (a generic anticipation of our Conclusion). Viktor Frankl's *Man's Search for Meaning* and Huss and Silverstein's *The Film Experience* are assigned as supplementary reading for these opening lectures. Any thorough, lucid exposition of the technical aspects of film, such as *The Cinema as Art* by Ralph Stephenson and J. R. Debrix (Penguin Books, revised edition, 1969) could be substituted for the latter.

All of the films studied in this work, as in the course, exhibit a basic visual similarity: some image of quest, usually the explicit metaphor of the road. Thus each shows man in his search for meaning. Our purpose is to allow each film to speak for itself initially so that its own visual and aural ingredients can provide us with the material for discussing spiritual meaning. All three dimensions of meaning—the personal, the social, and the religious—may be present in any given film, but one will usually predominate, and we have grouped the films accordingly. Implicit in every film are the three questions basic to man's quest, rooted in human consciousness: "Where do I come from? What am I? Where am I going?"

Finally, inasmuch as film expresses its meaning in visual terms, we ask the question whether there are not certain aspects of cinema technique that lend themselves more readily to a

Judaeo-Christian understanding of man's quest. There are, we feel, visual uses of physical reality and certain camera techniques that effectively constitute a medium of hope and affirmation for contemporary man, over against the celebration of presumption or the experience of despair.

The theological critic of contemporary culture, like Frankl's logotherapist,[18] is an eye specialist rather than a painter. The painter gives us an impression of the world as he sees it; the ophthalmologist strives to bring our vision back to the norm so that we can see life as it really is. By exposing the visual structures of a limited number of films, we hope that our reader will sharpen his own capacity for interpreting other films of quest and for discerning in them whatever meaning the form suggests. Our analogy, in the spirit of Frankl's, stresses obviously a difference of function rather than an evaluation of worth.

The director of film like the painter is of course a critic of culture too: He criticizes by creating a whole, though not wholly, new world of the imagination; the cultural commentator analyzes the constituent parts of the artistic whole so that the viewer will be aided in experiencing and evaluating for himself the world of the work. We go directly to the painting or the film, not of course to stay with the artist's world, but to allow his vision to direct ours to discover anew life's meaning, even if we must in Shakespeare's words "by indirections find directions out" (*Hamlet* II:i:65).

NOTES

1. *The Film Experience: Elements of Motion Picture Art* (New York: Dell Publishing Co., 1968), p. 2, our emphasis.

2. So Gerhard van Rad, Martin Buber, Johannes Metz, and a footnote in the RSV of the Bible.

3. See Erich Fromm, *You Shall Be as Gods* (Greenwich, Conn.: Fawcett Publications, Inc., 1969), pp. 132-33; Paul Ricoeur, *The Symbolism of Evil* (Boston: Beacon Press, 1969), pp. 72-74.

4. Josef Pieper, *Hope and History* (New York: Herder & Herder, 1969), p. 25; Gabriel Marcel, *Homo Viator* (New York: Harper & Row, 1962), p. 32.

5. *Hope and History*, p. 26.

6. Viktor Frankl, *Man's Search for Meaning* (New York: Washington Square Press, 1963), p. 63.

7. *You Shall Be as Gods*, p. 163.

8. *Building the Human* (New York: Herder & Herder, 1968), p. 83.

9. Ruben A. Alves, *A Theology of Human Hope* (Washington: Corpus Books, 1969), paraphrasing Marcuse, p. 22.

10. *Man Becoming* (New York: Herder & Herder, 1970), chap. 6, "Reinterpreting the Doctrine of God."

11. *Ibid.*, p. 195.

12. *Ibid.*

13. *Ibid.*, p. 196.

14. "Hope in a Posthuman Era," in *New Theology No. 5*, ed. Martin E. Marty and Dean G. Peerman (New York: Macmillan Co., 1968), pp. 86-87.

15. *Man's Search for Meaning*, p. 172.

16. *Ibid.*, p. 178.

17. *Ibid.*, p. 179.

18. *Ibid.*, p. 174.

Part One

THE PERSONAL DIMENSION

The search for meaning begins in the divided self. It sets us on a journey toward reconciliation that is marked by three essential experiences: (1) trusting and mastering the world, (2) being loved, and (3) loving. These experiences constitute the personal dimension of our search.

From the very beginning we need the other in order to become ourselves. We become ourselves in the other's presence.

Becoming a person is a process of involvement and detachment, of solitude and society, of embrace and release.

THE ROCKING-HORSE WINNER (1949)

Direction: Anthony Pelissier
Screenplay: Anthony Pelissier (based on a short story by D. H. Lawrence)
Photography: Desmond Dickinson

A collection of Bertolt Brecht's plays is aptly titled *Parables for the Stage*. It would not be difficult to gather a number of films into a volume entitled *Parables for the Screen*. *The Rocking-horse Winner* would certainly qualify for such a work. The short story by D. H. Lawrence on which the film is based begins like a parable: "There was a woman who was beautiful, who started with all the advantages, yet she had no luck."

"What *is* luck, mother?" she is asked one day by her young son. "It's what causes you to have money." Or what Uncle Oscar calls "filthy lucre." Call it what you will, Hester Grahame (Valerie Hobson) can never have enough of it. She has a small income, and so has her husband, but hardly enough for the social position they have to keep up. And so the whole house begins to whisper the unspoken phrase: *There must be more money! There must be more money!* The young Paul (John Howard Davies) hears it in the creaking of the stairs, in the swinging of a door, in the rocking of his hobby-horse.

Where will the money come from? Uncle Oscar can lend only so much. The father gambles, but he always loses, "unlucky" from the word *go*. In one of the film's most effective scenes (not to be found in the short story) Hester forces herself to go to a pawnshop and comes away humiliated. When she gets into a cab to return home, she finds that she will not have enough to pay the cabby. She tells him she has changed her mind and that she prefers to walk on such a lovely day. But to make sure he does not guess the real reason, she overpays him with all the money she has. As he calls after her, we see her, in a brief close-up, walk away in the full awareness of her folly.

PAUL: Aren't you lucky either, Mother?

23

> HESTER: I used to think I was, before I married.
> PAUL: Well, anyhow, *I'm* lucky.

And secretly he goes about proving it. Bassett, the gardener (John Mills), is very keen on horses. He keeps Paul posted with all the racing news. One day he places a bet for him, and that is the way it starts. When Uncle Oscar finds out about it, the boy has already won fifteen pounds.

> PAUL: We're all right when we're sure.
> OSCAR: But when are you sure?
> BASSETT: It's as if he had it from heaven.

The film never suggests that we should go beyond that "as if"; nevertheless, it successfully creates an air of mystery about the source of Paul's information. The interplay of light and dark, the gathering of shadows, even the cloud patterns, seem to posit a world beyond the visible or the natural, a preternatural world defying explanation.

And in the middle of that world stands the rocking-horse. To the little boy's mind, it is the rocking-horse that takes him "to where there is luck." He would mount his wooden steed and with whip in hand start on his mad journey, rocking in place, yet charging wildly into space, until at last he arrived. The camera makes the carved mouth and the glass eyes of the horse quicken with a life that almost matches the boy's frenzy. To see the horse is to see at a glance the beginning and the end of the journey.

And what will he do with all his winnings? Give it to mother, of course, so that the house will stop whispering. "I hate our house for whispering." But mother mustn't know how lucky he is, because that would end it all. So Uncle Oscar manages to get the money to her without telling her its true source. He deposits five thousand pounds with the family lawyer, who is then to say that it was left her by a relative.

With cold determination, the mother goes on a shopping spree as wild as Paul's ride on the horse. Surely now the whispering will stop. But it becomes more insistent than ever. "There must be *more* money! There *must* be more money!"

It frightens Paul terribly. The Grand National is upon them, but he is not "sure," and he loses a hundred pounds. Nor is he sure for the Lincoln either, and he loses another fifty. He becomes wild-eyed and strange. He *must* be sure for the Derby.

Two nights before the Derby, the mother is attending an important social event in town, when she is seized by a rush of anxiety. Returning home, she throws open the door of the boy's room and finds him plunging to the climax of a feverish ride on his wooden horse. "It's Malabar!" he screams. "It's Malabar!" And he falls unconscious. His mother does not know what to make of the boy's cry, but Uncle Oscar does. The bet is placed, and Paul wins eighty thousand pounds. He recovers only long enough to hear the good news, and to say to his mother: "Did I ever tell you? I *am* lucky!" And then he dies. The mother will not accept the money, and she has the rocking-horse burned. Standing behind the burning horse in the film's final shot, Hester seems to be burning *with* it, burning with the knowledge of her guilt. Indirectly, but nonetheless inescapably, she is responsible for her son's death.

Hester Grahame no doubt had for her son a certain instinctual love, but there was no time or place in her heart for the kind of love he needed and deserved as a person. The father was psychologically absent from the family. Unable to provide for it in the manner his wife demanded, and not strong enough to impose a more reasonable level of living, he disappears as both husband and father. The son, in a sense, is compelled to assume both these roles: He must provide for his mother, and the way he goes about it, plunging to a climax on his wooden horse, is not without its sexual overtones.

Hester had let herself be trapped by her own greed. She had come to define herself in terms of that first human experience whereby "this is mine" becomes "this is me." She takes to herself the blanket of the world and will not let go. The son, deprived of loving, is trapped into a desperate mode of expression.

The film implies entrapment in many ways. The house is enclosed by a fence. The characters are framed by windows, doors and gates, the stairway is narrow and steep, and one time the child peers through its railing as through prison bars. The box in which Paul's winnings are kept is coffin-like. The rock-ing-horse itself is, of course, an image of entrapment. Paul in-sists that by riding his horse he *gets there*, but in fact the horse gets nowhere. And like the wooden horse left by the Greeks for the Trojans, it appears to bear gifts but in fact brings destruc-tion. Paul's luck, like Greek fate, is ironic. So is Hester's Greek-sounding name: Hestia was the protectress of the domes-tic hearth.

Like all parables, *The Rocking-horse Winner* speaks to those who have ears. "The more we allow ourselves to be the servants of Having," says Gabriel Marcel, "the more we shall let ourselves fall prey to the gnawing anxiety which Having in-volves, the more we shall tend to lose not only the aptitude for hope, but even I should say the very belief, indistinct as it may be, of its possible reality."[1] If the search for meaning becomes a self-interment in *things*, self-realization becomes a hopeless task. Fundamental hope has to do with being, not with having.

O LUCKY MAN! (1973)

Direction: Lindsay Anderson
Screenplay: Lindsay Anderson and David Sherwin
Photography: Miroslav Ondricek

In the Preface to his screenplay, Lindsay Anderson claims that *O Lucky Man!* is "an organic development"[2] from his earlier work *If* (1968). The principal character is the same in both —Mick Travis played by Malcolm McDowell. Many of the same actors reappear, members of Anderson's talented troupe. But there the comparison may end, despite Anderson's disclaimer. *If* is generally taken as a revolutionary gesture, however humorous, ending as it does with a wide-eyed Mick gunning down the establishment from the roof of a boarding school. "Development does not imply repetition," Anderson writes, "and if this Mick starts as considerably more naive (and more conventionally ambitious) than the character in *If* . . . he ends up considerably wiser."[3]

The basic idea for the film, of a young salesman on his way to the top, comes, Anderson admits, from McDowell's own recollections of his youthful experiences selling coffee in Northeastern England. Travis's days as a coffee salesman, however, end apocalyptically a third of the way into the film; all that he has left to sell then is himself, if indeed this was not his product all along. Mick is convinced that luck is with him so he continues his relentless exposure to opportunity—with what success the film reveals only in its formal structures. The genesis of the film's title from *Coffee Man* to *Lucky Man* to *O Lucky Man!*, as described by David Sherwin in his "Diary of a Script," says a great deal indeed about the film's shifting levels of mood and meaning.

Anderson's young innocent begins a journey in the West of England that takes him to the Northeast, the North, the South, and finally to the East End of London. Single titles in white appear over a blackout, self-consciously announcing the quadrants

27

of Mick's quest as coterminus with the whole of England—a modern Everyman surveys the contemporary scene. The geographical titles are perhaps the most prominent of the film's formal devices, recalling the viewer's attention to the motif of journey while at the same time creating an initial impression of a closed system. The scenes within each geographical sequence of the film are often interrupted by blackouts, emphasizing the episodic character of the narrative as well as the equal significance of the scenes as parts of the whole.

The brief Prologue is a clever spoof of the Russian silent film that itself becomes a commentary on the body of the film. Malcolm McDowell as a peasant on a coffee plantation is caught stealing beans by the Foreman (the title reads "UNLUCKY") and is pronounced "GUILTY!" by the Judge. The sequence ends with a shot of the peasant's head jerking back, his mouth open in a scream, as off screen his hands are presumably being cut off by the Foreman's machete.

Within the overall geographical scheme of Mick's journey there are two opposing movements of quest, one of ascent and the other of descent. Mick's first stroke of luck at Imperial Coffee, being in the right place with the right smile when the Factory Chairman (Peter Jeffrey) announces Oswald's defection from the company's ranks, begins a pattern of ascent that takes Mick —circuitously of course—all the way to the top of the business world where by another stroke of good luck, witnessing his predecessor's suicide, he becomes the personal assistant of Sir James Burgess (Ralph Richardson), an unconscionable British tycoon. He irresponsibly connives with the denizens of power and is found "GUILTY!" of Sir James's crime, the sale of "honey" (a napalm-like substance) to the equally ruthless President of a new African nation. The establishment has such a vicious hold on wealth that there is no way for Mick to share the "beans" of success. The peasant had lost his hands, Mick loses his smile. After five years of hard labor, he emerges from prison a convert to the essential goodness of man. His journey into the depths of altruistic service, though, is a descent every bit as naive as his ascent to the realm of wealth and power. He is rejected by the derelicts at the bottom just as he had been by those at the top.

Still another formal device of the film is the reappearance of actors in different roles. "The choices were intuitive," Anderson asserts in his Preface, "never theoretical or 'programmed.' "[4] If the last qualification is intended as a general disclaimer of planned meaning, the device is potent enough to waive intentions. Ralph Richardson is the elderly tailor-philosopher Monty as well as the supercilious industrialist. Peter Jeffrey is both the Factory Chairman who invites Mick to bite into the apple of opportunity and the Prison Governor providing him with a collection of empty aphorisms to launch his crusade for goodness. Arthur Lowe is the fussy Works Manager at Imperial ("Always remember, gentlemen, that you are a failure in catering if you don't know what to do with your leftovers'), an oily provincial mayor, and the crafty black President of emerging Zingara. Rachel Roberts is the seductive Public Relations Officer for Imperial, Dr. Munda's white mistress, and a tenement mother who commits suicide (this episode was cut from the American release). And Mary MacLeod is the randy landlady of Sutherland House, the Vicar's wife, and the Salvation Army woman. Once the surprise of their reappearance has subsided, the viewer with Mick settles into an acceptance of the cyclic sameness of life, the recurring experience of *déjà vu* that supports Mick's circular journey.

The film's symbols are all related ironically to renewal; like the title they constitute a sardonic commentary on Anderson's vision of what life actually has to offer. The apple given by the Factory Chairman—and taken—is a humorous reminder of man's first invitation to presumption in Genesis. The gold suit from the aging tailor becomes a wedding garment for the fleeting new creation that follows the atomic catastrophe at the research facility. Our momentary new man—more a hungry babe in arms—must drink the milk of human kindness directly from the Vicar's wife's breast because the abundant fruits of the harvest are for God alone. Finally the Prison Governor's collection of what must be the world's greatest platitudes is as presumptuous a gift for the mind as Monty's suit had been for Mick's body. Moreover, the film's central episodes that are so mythic in structure—the apocalypse at the Atomic Research Establishment as well as the harvest thanksgiving at the paradisiacal vicarage—fit so comfortably into Anderson's vision of repetitive sameness that one must obviously conclude that neither end nor beginning is substantially different from middle.

A final formal device used with ironic effect is the detached and oblique commentary of the Alan Price songs. In a limbo setting in the darkness between episodes, Price's combo becomes a rock variation on the classical chorus:

> If you have a friend on whom you think you can rely—
>   You are a lucky man!
> If you've found the reason to live and not to die—
>   You are a lucky man!
> Preachers and poets and scholars don't know it,
> Temples and statues and steeples won't show it,
> If you've got the secret just try not to blow it—
>   Stay a lucky man!

Not until the film's final sequence, when a Mick much sobered by ascent as well as descent responds to an advertisement in Leicester Square ("STAR WANTED—TRY YOUR LUCK!"), is there any indication that he has "found the reason to live and not to die." In an audition hall, Lindsay Anderson himself appears (he is, coincidentally enough, casting *O Lucky Man!*), chooses Mick from the crowd, and orders him to smile.

> MICK: Why?
> DIRECTOR: Just do it.
> MICK: I'm afraid I can't smile without a reason.
> DIRECTOR (insistent): Smile!
> MICK (irritated now): What's there to smile about?
> DIRECTOR: Just do it!
> MICK: Why?
> DIRECTOR (gravely): Don't ask why.
> MICK (loudly): What's there to smile *about* . . . ?

Anderson pauses a moment, then strikes Travis across the face with his script. A faint smile begins to break across Mick's face as the camera zooms into a close-up and the title song is heard beginning for a final time. Is this the illumination that an earlier radio interview had promised? The illumination at the heart of

Za Zen—"to understand life, to be with life, to . . . get a feeling of life"—comes "suddenly" and "in many ways," the voice
is overheard saying. "Personally I can only say," Anderson
writes, "that [Mick] seems to me to arrive, after his journeying
through the world of illusion, at some kind of acceptance of reality. But acceptance is not conformism."[5] Critic David Wilson
rejoins: "But if all it means in *O Lucky Man!* is a woolly-mind-
ed coming to terms with the world as it is, it's a cold conclusion
from an angry man."[6]

Mick's reluctant smile suggests a realization that one must
question reality or at least question one's response to it. If Anderson's film seems to leave little opening for man's changing
the world, it is nonetheless emphatic that one cannot naively accept everything at face value. Anderson is apparently saying
that one must, in the final analysis, yield to the world's bidding.
It is not, however, the world of reasonable promise, described
by Viktor Frankl, but a cyclic system of repetitions. In the
film's last shot, shortly after Mick's "illumination," we see him
in celebration with the cast once again reaching out for illusions
—actually for a balloon—and hear for the first time a new stan-
za to the title song:

> And it's around and round and round and round and
>   round we go,
> And it's around the world in circles turning,
> Earning what we can . . .
> While others dance away the chance to light your day.

Mick's first line had indeed foreshadowed the conclusion; he
had told a fellow trainee at Imperial Coffee, "Do you realize
this Nigerian Coffee is being packed straight back to Nigeria?"

EAST OF EDEN (1954)

Direction: Elia Kazan
Screenplay: Paul Osborn (based on the novel by John Steinbeck)
Photography: Ted McCord

At least three times in John Steinbeck's novel *East of Eden* there are lengthy dialogues about the significance of the biblical story of Cain and Abel. Elia Kazan's film adaptation, less often than the novel but still as explicitly, uses the same myth to explain itself. After Cal-Cain (James Dean) has revealed their mother's identity to his brother Aron-Abel (Richard Davalos), precipitating Aron's flight into the army (and his eventual death, not disclosed in the film, though implied), the sheriff (Burl Ives) reflects self-consciously on the meaning of the incident: "And Cain went out and slew his brother, and God cursed him and he went into the land of Nod, east of Eden." His commentary is of course a conflation of words and ideas from the biblical passage (Genesis 4:1-16), ending with the phrase that gives the novel-film its title. The title suggests immediately that the dramatic action takes place "after the fall"; only the development of visual material can tell us that it also occurs "because of the fall."

The Genesis account of Cain and Abel (in the King James Version) ends with the verse: "And Cain went out from the presence of the Lord, and dwelt in the land of Nod, on the east of Eden." The Hebrew word *nod* means wanderer. Some modern translations say simply: "And he was a wanderer, east of Eden." Wandering is of course related metaphorically to quest; Cain is a mythic type of the searcher, Kazan's Cal his avatar.

Cal's quest for personal identity leads him to travel back and forth between the apparent polar extremes of his parents' worlds—between the Monterey of his mother (Jo Van Fleet) and the Salinas of his father (Raymond Massey), between the shrouded coastline of white slavery and the sunlit valley of righteousness. Cal knows with the instinct of the mythic wanderer that he will not discover who he is until he uncovers the mystery of his origin. The two worlds are actually the same though; Cal is rejected by both his parents, even if for different reasons. The film's first scene follows him in his pursuit of the woman Kate he knows to be his mother as she walks in apparent obscurity from the bank back to the source of her wealth, the house of pleasure she successfully manages; its opening shot of the fishing nets in Monterey harbor seems to suggest that any quest for acceptance must acknowledge the trap of sin into which man is born. From the scornful laughter of a woman's coldhearted world of business he cannot enter, the film cuts to Cal shivering atop the freight train that carries him back to his father's icy world of absolutely conditioned love he can never earn. Adam Trask explains his proposal for refrigerating lettuce for passage beyond the mountains. In the barnloft Cal sulks among the iceslabs, and we experience the chill of his alienation. When he overhears his brother's protestation of love for his girlfriend Abra (Julie Harris), his sense of rejection becomes a destructive tantrum and he hurls the ice down from the loft to liquefy at his father's feet. "You're bad, through and through bad," his father tells him later, persisting in a simplistic delusion that the darkness of his son's temperament is an innate blemish rather than the fruit of parental rejection.

Kazan following Steinbeck employs the mythic dimension to give epic stature to his narrative. And although the film foreshortens considerably the three-generation, East-to-West sweep of Steinbeck's novel, it nonetheless consciously strives to make the Trask family a paradigm of the American experience. The conflict between Cal and Aron must be seen against the backdrop of Adam Trask's American Puritanism just as the narrative of Cain and Abel finds its deepest interpretation in relation to the story of Adam and Eve as affirmation of a legacy of sin. The American experience, despite recurring prophecies of unconditioned progress, is not immune to the human condition; it too is lived "east of Eden."

The film like art in general draws its universal implications from the particular conflict. Why it asks are Cal and Aron at odds? Why does Cal like Cain insist, "I'm not my brother's keeper"? It is undoubtedly for the same fundamental reason that Americans fight against Germans. When the people of Salinas rise up against Gus Albrecht, their German neighbor, because their sons are going off to fight "the Huns," the concentric circles of the film's meaning broaden from family strife to global war to mankind in general. Why has brother always fought against brother? Every myth is thus somehow etiology, a study of causes, as well as an expression of a people's self-understanding. Both ancient and modern myths, it should be noted, distinguish between factual occurrences and expression of belief. Their truth is the truth of ideals, of vision, and of hope, not of history as we know it.

Kazan's *East of Eden* like the biblical narrative it is based on is concerned with the effect of acceptance and rejection on the quest for personal meaning. God favors Abel's sacrifice because he is a shepherd; he rejects Cain's offering of the fruit of the field. The Israelites, whose self-understanding the tale reflects, express their belief here in God's preference for the seminomadic life over the sedentary life of agriculture. The biblical question of life-style finds its curious equivalent in the film when Adam rejects Cal's birthday gift of money earned "off the war" in crop speculation. Beyond the support for a particular way of life, the story expresses a belief in the enduring mystery of God's favor by introducing the motif of the blessed younger son. The choice remains cloaked in mystery, yet it is clearly *God's* choice—presumably because he alone knows the inner value of the individual. The irony in *East of Eden* is that the human father, not God, makes the choice. Adam's self-righteous presumption is to claim God's knowledge of good and evil, but his facile Puritan logic yields only a simplistic distinction between black and white. Cal is like his mother Kate, but Kate leads a life of evil, and therefore Cal is "through and through bad"; whereas Aron, resembling his righteous father, is good.

There is for Steinbeck and Kazan yet another message in the biblical story, and this one is related to the Hebrew word *timshel* of Genesis 4:7. Despite his rejection of Cain's offering,

God speaks to him with assurance concerning the future: "If thou doest well, shalt thou not be accepted? And if thou doest not well, sin lieth at the door. And unto thee shall be his desire, and thou shalt [*timshel*] rule over him [i.e., sin]." As the King James Version translates it, *timshel* becomes "thou *shalt* master it," suggesting Cain's predestination to good. The American Standard Version renders it "thou *must* master it" which emphasizes God's command. It is only the final meaning though, of the three offered in the novel by the Chinese handyman, that affects the film's theme. The Hebrew word itself, Lee concludes, really means "thou *mayest* master it," thus insisting that despite rejection man has a choice.[7] He is free to overcome rejection and conquer evil. The meaning of Steinbeck's novel rests here; Kazan seems more concerned with the need for acceptance, with the dynamic tension that exists between the experience of love and one's active capacity for loving.

After Cal's destructive tantrum with the ice, Adam instructs his son; although the source of his "wisdom" is clearly Genesis 4:7, Adam gives *timshel* a characteristically facile twist. "A man has a choice, Cal. That's how he's different from an animal," he says. "You can make of yourself anything you want." Later, when Cal has precipitated the film's final tragedy, he confesses humbly, "It's awful not to be loved, it makes you mean," while remembering ironically his father's lesson: "Man has a choice!"

Yet Cal's rejection by his father especially is repeatedly emphasized—short of the final scene—by a visual composition of frames that shows him in angular juxtaposition to the physical world around him. He stands initially against the diagonal line of the ice shoot; we see his estrangement from his father in the opposition of lines. The diagonal in relation to Cal is a visual motif that cannot be ignored: the line of trees, the fence in front of the house, the roof of the shed, the steering wheel of the car, the row of beans in the field, the spoke of the ferris wheel, the roof of Abra's house, and the stairs outside his father's bedroom.

It is not, however, until the dying Adam expresses need for Cal that the boy knows he is loved and in being accepted can accept himself. "Do something for me," Adam asks, "get rid of that nurse." Cal tells Abra, "He said, 'Don't get anybody else. *You* stay with me!' " Adam chooses finally to accept his son as he is, and his protestation of dependence is a reasonably conditioned expression of love. For reasons we are not told but can only guess, he has discarded his fundamentalist discrimination of good and evil. Every man is a sad, but hope-filled mixture of good and evil; one accepts another despite the evil in him only if one acknowledges and transcends the evil in oneself. The film's final shot is unequivocal in its visual confirmation of Cal's justification through love. He is no longer at odds with reality; erect and self-assured, he blends perfectly with the proud upward thrust of his father's bedstead. And inasmuch as the camera throughout does indeed treat Cal lovingly,[8] *East of Eden* may intimate that the rejected are more lovable precisely because they have experienced evil.

SCARECROW (1973)

Direction: Jerry Schatzberg
Screenplay: Garry Michael White
Photography: Vilmos Zsigmond

Two drifters wait for a ride on a deserted Northern California road. The irony of the opening shot of *Scarecrow* is that the only thing that the two men share separates them as actually as if it were a chasm. Although they are apparently going in the same geographical direction, they move like strangers on opposite sides of the road. Max (Gene Hackman), just released from prison after serving time for assault, is on his way to Pittsburgh to open a hand car-wash, via Denver where his only relative, a sister, lives. An aggressive man who claims he has never loved anyone, he hides himself from genuine human contact in layers of protective clothing. Max's ostensible journey is a quest for modest financial stability.

Lion (Al Pacino), on the other hand, is a withdrawn, almost sheepish man, guilt-ridden for having abandoned his pregnant wife six years earlier. He has at last returned from the sea, remote from responsibility, hoping to reestablish contact with her again and to see his child for the first time. He carries with him on the road to Detroit an attractively wrapped gift for the child whose sex he does not even know. The neutral gift, a lamp, is a sadly ironic commentary on his years of neglect. Max and Lion are complementary characters, familiar from the patterns of modern drama, but only superficially related to other famous pairs. Unlike the irreconcilable dualism of Samuel Beckett's Estragon and Vladimir in *Waiting for Godot* and Tom Stoppard's more recent Rosencrantz and Guildenstern, Max and Lion meld gradually into a union that is both affecting and inspiring.

Slowly, imperceptibly, they are drawn together by their common need as their journey unfolds. Despite his obsessive guilt, Lion manages to begin his reconciliation with life in modest but significant ways. Max insists that Lion is the first person who has ever really done anything for him: Lion gave him his last cigarette and, more importantly, taught him to laugh. Although the beauty of Schatzberg's vision of the power of selfless giving lies in the simplicity of his understated images, he nonetheless explains the meaning of his title, though certainly without offense. Lion tells Max the story of farmer Jones who discovers the peculiar effectiveness of scarecrows. They do not really scare the crows, farmer Jones notices, they make them laugh and in that way distract them from the crops. Lion is indeed the scarecrow who in helping Max to laugh at situations he cannot change provides him with a meaningful sublimation for his aggression.

Max's reunion with his sister Coley (Dorothy Tristan) is more than just a stopover on their journey East. It is a hopeful celebration of discovered friendship as well as its first crucial test. Lion is attracted to Coley, and Max meets and likes her arty friend Frenchy (Anne Wedgeworth). Coley's junk yard is a facetious reminder of the past both Max and Lion have escaped from. The four make plans for the future, after Max has retrieved his savings from the Pittsburgh bank—typical of man's illusory engagement with life in comparison with the growth of the essential bond between the men.

A farewell party turns into a drunken brawl, and Max and Lion are sentenced to thirty days at the county work farm for disturbing the peace. When Lion rebuffs the homosexual advances of a fellow inmate named Riley (Richard Lynch) and is brutally beaten by him, Max shows how in the cause of friendship aggression becomes justifiable outrage. Max avenges Lion, but the fury of his retributive action is minimized by the singular and effective use of a far shot that makes the combatants seem like ants; it is as if we are told what happens but are spared the sight of its violence.

Released from prison, the pair resume their journey to Detroit. Lion's broken nose and innumerable stitches give his countenance the patched sadness of a scarecrow's. The more literally he resembles one the less apparently he seems capable of making anyone laugh. Racked by years of guilt and now physically shaken, Lion is ill-prepared for the encounter with his estranged wife, Annie (Penny Allen). His first and only overture is to call cautiously from a booth near her house. Annie peppers her rejection—and apparently conceals her own infidelity—with lies and recriminations. In full view of their healthy young son, she claims that, because she had no one to help her after falling on ice, he died at birth without baptism and is forever deprived of heaven. Visibly shocked, though unable to admit Annie's tirade, Lion tells Max that she is happily remarried; they can celebrate before leaving together for Pittsburgh since he declines to intrude upon her new life.

The scene is thus set for their bond to be permanently sealed. Schatzberg's typically quiet symbolism captures the poignancy of Lion's moment of utter need. In a nearby park, Lion, with a stare emptied more by shock than from drinking, gathers a stranger's child into his arms and walks into a fountain in a gesture of expiation for his unbaptized son. Before Max reaches him, Lion has slipped into the catatonic state that draws a final commitment from his friend; Max will return from Pittsburgh to sacrifice his savings for Lion's return to health.

Hitchhiking, hopping freight trains, and walking, Max and Lion go from northern California to Denver and finally to Detroit. Although Max's physical journey (to Pittsburgh) is not completed in the course of the film, his spiritual journey has opened possibilities for him beyond imagination, certainly beyond his desire. Despite his earlier insulation, Max responds to life's demands in the person of Lion and has at the film's end discovered his true self through the love of another.

The Production Notes issued by Warner Brothers when the film was released speak knowledgeably of the deeper meanings of the American experience of the road:

Drifters have been wandering the American landscape lending legend and romance as they borrowed spare change and a night's lodging throughout the heritage and folklore of this country since its birth. The loners were among the best and worst of us. Call them what we will, the hoboes, the tramps, the bums, hippies,

backpackers, bikers or thumb-trippers, the people of
the road have always been true Americana, heralded
in story and song even before the trails were strung
with rails and sleepy country roads were paved for the
super-speeders.

The journey, we have come to understand on an even deeper
level, is an archetypal reminder to man that life itself is a quest
for meaning.

LA STRADA (1954)

Direction: Federico Fellini
Screenplay: Federico Fellini, Ennio Flaiano, and Tulio Pinelli
Photography: Otello Martelli

Gelsomina's face, with lips made of putty, eyes bulging, brow furrowed, and hair spilling over it like straw, is a mirror for catching spirits. You see loneliness there, the need to love and be loved, the wonder of things, hope and despair. You even see a passion for meaning. And perhaps the wings of *that* spirit gather all the others in.

There is one scene in *La Strada* in which the passion for meaning is poignantly visible. It is the scene between Gelsomina (Giulietta Masina) and the Fool (Richard Basehart) that takes place at the close of the circus in Rome. Gelsomina, a simple-minded imp of a girl, has been brought to Rome by Zampano (Anthony Quinn), an itinerant stunt-man who paid her mother ten thousand lira for her services. Callous and obtuse, he teaches her a few tricks to assist him in his act, which consists in breaking an iron chain with the muscles of his chest. Ordinarily, he performs on the road (*la strada*), but decides to join the circus for the winter. There they meet the Fool, who makes fun of Zampano and provokes him into drawing a knife on him. Zampano is jailed for the night, and that night the Fool approaches Gelsomina. She is miserable. Zampano is a brute. He treats her like dirt. "Oh, why was I born?" she cries. And then the Fool tells her the parable of the stone.

> THE FOOL: Of course . . . if *you* didn't stay with him, who would? Everything in this world is good for . . . for something. Take this stone, for instance.
> GELSOMINA: Which one?
> THE FOOL: Uh, this one—it doesn't matter which. This one, too, it has a purpose, even this little pebble.
> GELSOMINA: What's it good for?

THE FOOL: If I knew that, I would be God. But if this stone is useless, then everything is, even the stars. You too, you have a purpose too. You with your artichoke head.

Her purpose is to stay with Zampano, to take care of him, to set him free from the bondage of his own nature, to love him, to make him love her, to save him. When she takes the pebble in her hand, this is surely what she sees, even if she cannot say so. What she says instead is: "Me, I'm going to set fire to everything! That will teach him. If I weren't the one to stay with him, who would? Huh?"

Her sense of vocation is fortified by the words of a nun she meets on the way: "We change convents every two years, so as not to forget the most important thing: God. We travel, you and I. I follow my Husband, and you follow yours." Gelsomina sees now the road she must take. Her face is alight with hope. "To love anybody is to expect something from him," says Gabriel Marcel, "something which can neither be defined nor foreseen; it is at the same time to make it possible for him to fulfill this expectation."[9] Gelsomina does everything in her power to make it possible, but Zampano never changes—until one day on a lonely road he comes upon the Fool and beats him in a cold fury. The Fool looks at his shattered watch and dies. Zampano makes the unintentional murder look like an automobile accident and flees from the scene with Gelsomina.

Gelsomina falls into a stupor. She whimpers constantly and can speak no word but the Fool's name. Conscience-striken, unable to endure the girl's crying, he abandons her on the road. Years pass before he learns of her death in a seaside town. That night, alone on the beach, he falls on his knees and weeps.

"In each of my films," says Fellini, "there is a character who goes through a crisis. It seems to me that the best atmosphere with which to underline this moment of crisis is a beach or a piazza, at night; silence, the emptiness of night, or the feeling that the sea is close by, brings the character into relief."[10] Zampano is surely such a character; his journey leads inevitably to the sea. Throughout the film, a very close relationship between Gelsomina and the sea is established, so much so that the sea itself becomes an evocative symbol of her. We meet her fo. the first time by the sea. Before she goes off with Zampano, she kneels beside it as if to confide in it. Later, when she and Zampano pause by the sea, she runs up to it with joy in her face. (Zampano pisses in it.) She calls upon the sea to witness her "marriage" to him: "Once I would have wanted to leave; now you are my country." At the end of the film, therefore, when Zampano falls on his knees by the sea, she is surely there. It is as if she has at last fulfilled her vocation: She has made of him a human being.

In *La Strada* Fellini takes what he calls an "old problem" and places it in one of those special worlds of which he is master, so that there is no longer anything "old" about it at all. It's the "old problem of communication, the desperate anguish to be *with*, the desire to have a real, authentic relationship with another person."[11] If at the end of the film we sense that anguish so profoundly, it is because now Zampano feels it too, and we are grateful for that, for his sake, and for Gelsomina's sake, and we dare to hope for him as she had dared. We are not brought to this depth of feeling inevitably through a succession of scenes, each giving rise to the next, as in the linear development of a dramatic plot. It comes upon us gratuitously—like grace—just as it comes upon Zampano.

The structure of the film is open to grace. People can walk in and out of it and still belong. The nun who compared Gelsomina's vocation to hers is like that. And what shall we say about that episode—gratuitous yet integral—of the idiot child that Gelsomina comes upon by chance? There is a feast going on at a farm, and Gelsomina, who likes people and who wants to stay with them and take part in the general merriment, is led off by a host of children to see the idiot boy. He peers at her out of his bedclothes. Eyes popping with awe and curiosity, she comes up right next to his face. It is a memory from Fellini's own childhood. "I probably used it to give Gelsomina an exact awareness of solitude."[12]

Grace comes through the Fool too. Traditionally, in drama, the fool makes people aware of other dimensions to "old problems." In *La Strada*, the Fool's act is to walk a tight-rope between heaven and earth, wearing wings and eating a plate of spaghetti. By image, as well as by word, he reminds us that the ultimate meaning of man reaches between two worlds.

IKIRU (1952)

Direction: Akira Kurosawa
Screenplay: Hideo Oguni, Shinobu Hashimoto, and Akira
  Kurosawa
Photography: Asaichi Nakai

Akira Kurosawa's *Ikiru* is one of those visually precise
films whose end is perfectly implied in its beginning. Its opening
shot is an X-ray of a gastric cancer. Our "hero," the narrator's
voice informs us, knows nothing of it. The cut is directly to the
subject himself, Kanji Watanabe (Takashi Shimura), engaged in
a routine gesture—looking at his watch—that will later erupt
with significance. We thus see the inside of the man before we
see the man himself. The source of Mr. Watanabe's disease is
physical; his real illness, though, is spiritual and it is only *within*
that he will ultimately discover its cure.

After cutting from cancer to man, the film cuts back to
reveal the source of Watanabe's spiritual death. Chief of the
Citizens' Section at City Hall, he is buried in the debris of petty
officialdom. The piles of undisturbed papers are less penetrable
even than marble; they are the depersonalized winding sheets of
governmental bureaucracy. The narrator explains somewhat
needlessly, "He is like a corpse, and actually he has been dead
for the past twenty-five years" (the term of his municipal service). A young office girl will tell him later that she had nicknamed him "the mummy."

The following scene, a series of short wipe-punctuated
shots, explains why the system destroys. Although the malfunc-
tion of the social order is clearly a target of Kurosawa's, with
relevance to our subsequent investigation of the social dimension of man's quest, he has nonetheless focused his camera on
one man's capacity to unravel a thread of personal meaning in
the face of death despite the hopelessly tangled knot of official
red tape. The scene is also important to the narrative structure
of the film because it anticipates the specific design of Wa-

tanabe's response to life. A group of housewives, complaining about the potential health hazard from a sump in their neighborhood, request that it be drained and converted perhaps into a playground. Although they approach a clearly marked window —"THIS IS YOUR WINDOW. IT IS YOUR LINK WITH THE CITY HALL. WE WELCOME BOTH REQUESTS AND COMPLAINTS"—they are sent on a rapid tour of related offices only to return without success to the place where they started. No one will accept responsibility for the problem! They have completed the closed circle of bureaucratic futility.

In the sharply edited transition to the visual explanation of the opening X-ray, we see the Deputy Chief (Kamatari Fujiwara) looking at the Chief's desk, an empty desk, then Watanabe in a hospital corridor. A talkative patient unknowingly prepares him to diagnose his own symptoms. The doctor skirts the truth; Watanabe is nonetheless numbed by the encounter. The introductory sequence ends as it began with the X-ray of his stomach. Ironically only the announcement of death seems to be stimulus enough to launch Mr. Watanabe's quest for life.

If the end of *Ikiru* is implied in its beginning, the film's most telling structural device is its division into two parts. From Mr. Watanabe's realization that he has only a half year to live until the moment of suggested though undisclosed meaning, a month elapses and Watanabe's panicked experimentation with life's possibilities is shown directly. The dividing cut is to a picture of Watanabe on a funeral altar while the narrator announces, "Five months later our hero died." The second, though shorter portion of the film is devoted to the wake and to our indirect discovery, through the jigsaw pattern of his mourners' often reluctant recollections, of the precise nature of Watanabe's adjustment to living. The irony of Kurosawa's device is that the lived present of the first part reveals a dead past whereas the second half's reconstructed past discloses what Watanabe's rich, though limited, future was like. Kurosawa applies perfectly the artistic principle stated in the nighttown sequence. As Watanabe and the writer oggle a striptease, the latter comments, "Oh, that's not art. A striptease isn't art. It is too direct. It is more direct than art."

The first part of *Ikiru* describes the stages of Watanabe's response to the imminence of death. Outside of the hospital, he rushes stunned down an unnaturally quiet street. Only when we hear the harsh screech of a passing truck that nearly runs him down do we realize the shot has till then been completely silent. With Watanabe we are made deaf through shock which has driven him so deeply within himself that only the louder noises of the street can pierce his consciousness.

His first desire, when shock subsides, is to share his hated secret with his son, Mitsuo (Nobuo Kaneko), the only family he has. But Mitsuo, concerned only for himself and his wife, is incapable of understanding his father's muted trauma. In a magnificent sequence, intercut with illuminating flashbacks and poignantly unified by sound overlap, Kurosawa conveys Watanabe's isolation from his son in a painfully abortive gesture of communication. We see a full shot of Watanabe kneeling in his room before the shrine of his dead wife, a close-up of her picture, a close-up of Watanabe looking at it, a close close-up of the picture, then a dissolve to a rear view of the hearse through the rain-flecked windshield of a moving car. Young Mitsuo complains to his father as the hearse turns the corner, "Hurry. We must hurry. Mother is leaving us behind." Their present estrangement has its roots in the past. Watanabe, we learn, decided not to remarry so that he could devote himself exclusively to raising his son. But when Mitsuo had an attack of appendicitis while playing baseball, his father protested that he was unable to remain with him during the operation because he had "some things to do." Obligations of this sort, we know from Watanabe's record as a civil servant, only conceal his inability to love. Since they have never apparently been close, Mitsuo's departure for the war merely adds physical distance to the spiritual separation they have always known.

Watanabe's reverie is interrupted at one point by his son calling, "Father." He hastens to climb the stairs to his son, but Mitsuo does not want to share—only to instruct. He asks his father to "lock up." The downward angle of the camera captures Watanabe's retreat in near despair, as if into a hole. The walls and ceiling are not sufficient to express his loneliness. There is no solace for him through family. The sequence ends, with Watanabe weeping under his covers, on an ironic cut to a citation on the wall commending him for his "twenty-five years of devoted service."

The past raked and found wanting, Watanabe decides to give himself to a life of pleasure (drawing from the bank the money his son had selfishly hoped to use for a new house), and with the writer he has met launches into the city of night. The Faustian futility of seeking satisfaction in sensual gratification is emphasized, perhaps facetiously, when the writer refers to himself as Mephistopheles and notices a black dog at his feet. In the melee of streets riotous with pleasure-seekers, Watanabe loses his hat and buys a new one. Whatever symbolic significance this change has at this time must be limited to his developing realization that there is no meaning for him, only added pain, in indulgence of the senses.

The last stage of Watanabe's quest, his attempt to give himself to someone, bears fruit beyond anticipation. Quite by chance he befriends a young girl from the city office (Miki Odagiri), the one who confesses to having nicknamed him "the mummy." His gestures of friendship are innocent and simple: he gives her new stockings that she so badly needs and signs her papers of resignation so that she at least can satisfy her desire to flee the boredom of bureaucracy. She is too young though to be able to respond to his need for affection. Their last meeting, appropriately set in a coffee shop frequented by youth, becomes ironically the delayed beginning of Watanabe's life. In dialogue that bears careful scrutiny, the girl unwittingly offers him an answer to life's challenge.

> WATANABE: You . . . just to look at you makes me feel better. It warms this . . . mummy heart of mine. And you are so kind to me. No, that's not it. You are so young, so healthy. No, that's not it either. You are so full of life. And me . . . I'm envious of that. If only for one day I would like to be like you before I die. I won't be able to die, somehow, unless I can be. Oh, I want to do something. Only you can show me. I don't know what to do. I don't know how to do it. Maybe you don't know ei-

ther, but, please, if you can, show me how to be like
you.
GIRL: I don't know . . .
WATANABE: How can I be like you?
GIRL: All I do is work—and eat. That's all.
WATANABE: Really?
GIRL: Yes, really, I just make toys like this. (She
puts a mechanical rabbit on the table in front of
them; she works in a toy factory now.) And that is
all I do, but I feel as though I am friends with all
the children in Japan. Mr. Watanabe, why don't
you do something like that, too?
WATANABE: What could I do at the office?
GIRL: Well, that's true. Then resign and find something else.
WATANABE: It is too late . . . No, it isn't too
late. It isn't impossible . . . I *can* do something if I
really want to.

In the commotion of a nearby celebration, Watanabe, with a
glow of realization on his face, grabs the rabbit and rushes
down the stairs against the ascent of the pretty girl whose gathered friends sing "Happy Birthday." The strains of this song,
with obvious significance, overlap the cut to Watanabe's office
where he rummages through his desk, discovers the neglected
petition for the neighborhood playground, and rushes back out
into the rain as the baffled deputy chief follows him to the door.
It is at this point that Kurosawa ends the first half of his film.

With the exception of the explanatory flashbacks and a
brief final scene, the entire second half of the film occurs in Watanabe's room which has been rendered almost unrecognizable
by its funeral trappings. The family and fellow workers have
gathered for the wake; his colleagues attempt to resolve the
enigma of his final days and the peculiar circumstances of his
death. The visual rhythm of this final prolonged sequence is as
regular as the flow of waves onto a beach, though by no means
as fast. The discussion of the mourners yields suggestive clues
despite their general reluctance to admit Watanabe's gain; intimation fades into confirming flashback; the mourners return,
curiously quiet at first as if assimilating the new insight, gradually stirring into new discovery.

Everyone knows that Watanabe died on a park swing in the snow. Did he freeze to death, or was it suicide? No, he died of cancer and he knew he had it. But why on the park swing? The park was his gift to the children of the neighborhood; he achieved the goal alone. But the Department of Parks creates parks, not the Deputy of the Citizens' Section, the others protest. No, Watanabe—with incredible perseverance—overcame bureaucratic inertia and forced the completion of the project. He even ignored the base threat of the tavern lobbyists, "Do you value your life?" Because Watanabe had no life left to value, he could sacrifice it completely for others. A policeman returns Watanabe's battered hat and offers the mourners a final, touching vignette of his death. He had seen him swinging in the snow and heard him singing a song; he seemed content— and even happy! Although the song may seem plaintive, its lyrics, heard in a context of visual serenity, so typical of Japanese art, point directly to the film's message of urgency.

> Life is so short,
> Fall in love, dear maiden,
> While your lips are still red,
> And before you are cold,
> For there will be no tomorrow.
> Life is so short,
> Fall in love, dear maiden,
> While your hair is still black,
> And before your heart withers,
> For today will not come again.

Man's existence, Kurosawa reminds us, is limited: The only way for him to redeem the time is to make the most urgent use of the day that is given to him. The film's choice of physical reality, however, calls for meaning beyond mere doing as some existentialist interpreters seem to have reduced it. Donald Richie, for example, even while admitting that "it is quite possible Kurosawa would disagree with this interpretation,"[13] insists that Watanabe's lesson is that "a man *is* what he *does*."[14] "The meaning," Richie explains, "is that Watanabe has discovered himself through *doing*. Perhaps without even grasping the profound truth he was acting out, he behaved as though he believed that it is action alone which matters; that a man is not his thoughts, nor his wishes, nor his intentions, but is simply what he does. Watanabe discovered a way to be responsible for others, he found a way to vindicate his death and, more important, his life. He found out what it means *to live*."[15] The title itself, *Ikiru*, it should be noted, is an intransitive verb meaning "to live."

In the final analysis, though, even Kurosawa's intentions must yield to what the film itself says through the physical reality it celebrates. The choice of a park for children as the goal of Watanabe's action as well as of the memento box containing only his clock and the girl's rabbit, given such prominent display at the conclusion of the wake, demands some statement about the object of the action. One must work and thus live *for* others. Moreover, the film's final shot of the disappointed clerk passing the playground—the one fellow worker who had understood and defended Watanabe during the wake, yet was himself alone unable to overcome the inertia that the Citizens' Section immediately slipped back into—would seem to suggest that it is only when one's own death is seen as imminent that one comes to realize fully life's limitation and its urgent call to meaning. That a drama about death should ultimately be about the meaning of life is not a paradox unfamiliar to the Christian world.

WILD STRAWBERRIES (1957)

Direction: Ingmar Bergman
Screenplay: Ingmar Bergman
Photography: Gunnar Fischer

It is possible to dream oneself into reality. The experience of Isak Borg in *Wild Strawberries* can be so described. By dream and daydream, a day's trip becomes a life's journey, an excursion into the past becomes a launching into the future, a plunging into the depths of his own soul generates the movement upward.

Looking over the progress of the day, the 76-year-old Isak (Victor Sjöström) writes in his diary: "I was beginning to see a remarkable causality in this chain of unexpected, entangled events."[16] Once again, as in Fellini's *La Strada*, the film is so structured that its causality is not to be found in a succession of scenes, each giving rise to the other, all of them moving toward an inevitable conclusion. Isak never names the causality he detects in the "unexpected" events of the day. One may call it, tentatively, the causality of grace.

Isak Borg, doctor of medicine, has been awarded an honorary degree. He must travel to Lund to receive it. His son Evald (Gunner Björnstrand) lives there, married to Marianne (Ingrid Thulin), but they have no children. Their marriage is not going well, and Marianne has come to stay with Borg in the hope of getting him to help, a hope that he unequivocally disappoints. Now she wants to drive back with him to Lund. His original plan had been to fly to Lund with his housekeeper Agda (Jullan Kindahl), who has served him faithfully for forty years, but apparently a terrifying dream the night before prompts him to change his mind.

In that dream, he finds himself on a deserted street under a clock with no hands. To his joy, he sees someone standing on the street corner. He rushes up to him and touches his arm. The man turns; he has no face under his soft hat, he collapses at

Isak's feet as if made of dust. Isak hears a tolling of bells and sees a funeral procession wending its way through the streets. Rounding a turn, a wheel of the horse-drawn hearse catches on a lamppost. It comes loose, rolling toward him with a loud clatter. The coffin slips out of the hearse and falls into the street. A hand sticks out of it. When Isak draws near, the dead hand clutches his arm and pulls him down toward the coffin. Struggling helplessly, he sees the corpse. It is himself.

This awareness of his own death stands at the beginning of all those "unexpected, entangled events" of the day. Like Everyman, he comes face to face with Death and is commanded, as it were, to go on a pilgrimage "which he in no wise can escape." Enroute to Lund, he retraces the steps of his own life. "You are an old egotist," Marianne says outright. "You are completely inconsiderate and you have never listened to anyone but yourself." She berates him for being "stinking rich" and still insisting that his son Evald pay back, at a rate of five thousand per year, the money he lent him to complete his studies in medicine.

> ISAK: A bargain is a bargain, my dear Marianne. I know that Evald understands and respects me.
> MARIANNE: That may be true, but he also hates you.

They make two stops on the way to Lund, both of them visits into the past. The first is to an old house by the sea, where Isak had spent the summer for the past twenty years of his life with his family. While Marianne goes for a swim, Isak sits alone in the wild strawberry patch and peoples the scene with his memory. He sees his cousin Sara (Bibi Andersson), the girl he had intended to marry, picking strawberries. His brother Sigfrid (Per Sjöstrand) comes up to her, taunts her about Isak, and in forcing a kiss upon her knocks over the basket of wild strawberries. Confused and excited, Sara will later admit to herself that Isak is a prig, and she ends up marrying Sigfrid.

Isak's second stop is a visit to his mother. At ninety-six, she has survived her husband and nine of her children. Isak is the only one left. None of her grandchildren has ever come to

visit her. She has never seen her fifteen great-grandchildren. She
admits, of course, that she is tiresome. "And then I have another fault. I don't die." Her memory plays tricks on her. She
thinks Marianne is Isak's wife Karin, who has been dead for
many years. "I refuse to talk with her. She has hurt us too
much."

But actually it was Isak who hurt Karin. His indifference,
his condescension, his lack of love drove her to adultery. He
relives the scene of one of her adulteries in a dream he has while
sleeping in the car. He finds himself in an amphitheater in
which he is required to take an examination. What is a doctor's
first duty? He cannot remember. He has to be told: "A doctor's
first duty is *to ask forgiveness*." When he wakes, he confides in
Marianne.

> ISAK: The last few months I've had the most peculiar
>   dreams. It's as if I'm trying to say something to
>   myself which I don't want to hear when I'm awake.
> MARIANNE: And what would that be?
> ISAK: That I'm dead, although I live.

Marianne reacts violently to this statement, and she tells
him why: His son Evald has said the very same thing. The most
recent threat to her marriage to Evald came when she revealed
to him that she was pregnant. She wants to have the child, he
insists that she abort it: "It's absurd to live in this world, but it's
even more ridiculous to populate it with new victims. . . . Personally, I was an unwelcome child in a marriage which was a
nice imitation of hell. Is the old man really sure that I'm his
son?" When Marianne tells him that he is wrong not to want
the child, he claims there is nothing that is right or wrong; one
functions according to one's needs. His need is, by his own admission, to be dead. "Absolutely, totally dead."

Now, sitting next to Isak in the car, having just left his
mother and soon to see Evald again, Marianne voices a strange
fear:

> I thought, here is his mother. A very ancient woman,
> completely ice-cold, in some ways more frightening
> than death itself. And here is her son, and there are

light-years of distance between them. And he himself says that he is a living death. And Evald is on the verge of becoming just as lonely and cold—and dead. And then I thought that there is only coldness and death, and death and loneliness, all the way. Somewhere it must end.

The Borgs—they pass like a procession of icebergs, one reflected in the other. Here we have the essence of Bergman's dramatic structure. While the overall structure of the film is a literal journey, the inner journey proceeds by what Francis Fergusson calls "the analogy of action."[17] Or, to use Henry James's phrase, we are constantly shifting "from reflector to reflector" throughout the film, each reflector mirroring the central action, revealing it from various (ironically different) angles. The central action is, of course, Isak Borg's—the attempt to face the frozen misery of generations, to move against the ice in his own heart.

Three other encounters serve as reflectors in the film. The first encounter is deliberately juxtaposed to his memory of the Sara he lost. A young girl rouses him from his reverie: she and two companions are hitchhiking to Italy. Her name is also Sara, and she is played by the same actress who plays the Sara of his youth. Like the first Sara, she is engaged to one man (Anders, who is studying to be a minister) but is also attracted to another (Viktor, a medical student who does not believe in God). Clearly, the three of them mirror his youth. Once, in a dream, he had said to his Sara: "It wasn't always like this. If only you had stayed with me. If only you could have had a little patience."

The second encounter is a close call. Rounding a blind curve, they almost collide with a reckless driver. Isak's car skids to a stop, but the other car rolls over into a ditch. A man and a woman crawl out of it unhurt, in the midst of a violent quarrel. "I was just going to hit my husband," the woman says, "when that curve appeared." Isak gives them a lift in his already crowded car, but they continue to tear at each other with such malice that Marianne insists they get out and walk. Later, Isak will say: "It reminded me of my own marriage." And Marianne: "I didn't want Evald and me to become like . . ."

The third encounter is brief but deserves mention because it shows us a man and woman apparently content in their marriage and gives us a glimpse of Isak as he might have been. Isak stops for gas in a region where he began his medical practice. The gas-station attendant (Max von Sydow) recognizes him and calls to his wife: "Here you see Dr. Borg himself in person. This is the man that Ma and Pa and the whole district still talk about. The world's best doctor." Almost to himself, Isak says: "Perhaps I should have remained here." It may be that in the service of others the ice would not have formed. But earlier Marianne had said to him: "Everyone depicts you as a great humanitarian. We who have seen you at close range, we know what you really are."

At journey's end the honorary degree is conferred upon Isak Borg. So, too, a touch of grace. When they had stopped to rest at a roadside inn that afternoon, Isak had dreamily begun to recite a poem in order to end an argument between Sara's two companions.

> ISAK: "Where is the friend I seek everywhere? Dawn is the time of loneliness and care. When twilight comes . . ." What comes after that?
> MARIANNE: "When twilight comes I am still yearning."

Isak, in the twilight of his life, is still yearning. Is there fire enough to thaw the ice in his heart?

> ISAK: "I see His trace of glory and power, In an ear of grain and the fragrance of flower . . ."
> MARIANNE: "In every sign and breath of air. His love is there."

Is it also in the "unexpected, entangled events" of the day? Is the "remarkable causality" that Isak sees there a causality of grace? Certainly, it can be said that the ice begins to thaw. To be spiritually dead, as he saw it, was to be buried in his own frozen self; to be spiritually alive, then, is to go out to others. Unlike Watanabe in *Ikiru*, he cannot go out to just anybody. After all, as a doctor, he had served others well, wearing his humanitarian mask. No, for Isak, it is necessary to go out to those for whose misery he is largely responsible. To Agda, of course, the housekeeper who has tolerated him for forty years, but especially to his own son. In a quietly effective scene, he expresses concern for Evald's marriage to Marianne and tries to convey to him that the loan he made him is to be considered a gift.

In the final sequence of the film, Isak, alone in his bed, wanders back in memory to the wild strawberry patch. Wild strawberries were used in an earlier film (*The Seventh Seal*) as a symbol of simple humanity, of sharing, of involvement with others—of the very qualities that Isak had never cultivated. He had let them instead spill out of his life ("Isak, darling, there are no wild strawberries left"). But now the ground has thawed, they will bloom again, and he will find a few and hold them in the cup of his hands. But are they really enough? "When twilight comes I am still yearning."

NOTES

1. *Homo Viator*, p. 61.
2. Lindsay Anderson and David Sherwin, *O Lucky Man!* (London: Plexus Publishing Ltd., 1973), p. 8.
3. *Ibid.*
4. *Ibid.*
5. *Ibid.*, pp. 8-9.
6. David Wilson, "O Lucky Man!" *Sight and Sound* 42:3 (Summer 1973), 129.
7. Cf. John Steinbeck, *East of Eden* (New Bantam Edition, 1970), pp. 310-11, 349-50, 597-98.
8. "Maybe his father doesn't love him," Pauline Kael demurs, "but the camera does, and we're supposed to. . . . A boy's agonies should not be dwelt on so lovingly: being misunderstood may easily become the new and glamorous lyricism" (*I Lost It at the Movies*, p. 49).
9. *Homo Viator*, p. 49.
10. Gilbert Salachas, *Federico Fellini, An Investigation Into His Films and Philosophy* (New York: Crown Publishers, 1969), p. 115.
11. Quoted in *The Filmviewer's Handbook* by Emile G. McAnany, S.J., and Robert Williams, S.J. (Glen Rock, N.J.: Paulist Press, 1965), p. 106.
12. Salachas, *Federico Fellini*, p. 10.
13. Donald Richie, *The Films of Akira Kurosawa* (Berkeley, Calif.: University of California Press, 1970), p. 95.

14. *Ibid.*, p. 94.

15. *Ibid.*

16. All quotations of *Wild Strawberries* are taken from *Four Screenplays of Ingmar Bergman*, trans. by Lars Malmstrom and David Kushner (New York: Simon & Schuster, 1960).

17. *The Idea of a Theater* (Princeton, N.J.: Princeton University Press, 1949), chap. 4, "Hamlet, Prince of Denmark: The Analogy of Action."

Part Two

THE SOCIAL DIMENSION

Our relationship to others is a spiraling outward into a world of ever-increasing complexity, a world that both invites and threatens, a world of communion in which we can be at home with ourselves and yet not be alone.

The family, the neighborhood, the city, the nation, the world—these are the structures for community, and yet each one can become a prison.

Technology has put into the hands of man a power to create new forms of freedom, new images of the future—so long as it remains technology. When it becomes technologism, when it ceases to be a tool and becomes instead a "savior," it envelops, conditions, and determines man. Man becomes one-dimensional, a part of the total technological system.

If that system is threatened, it must preserve itself at all costs; it engages in that abuse of technology called modern warfare.

ALICE'S RESTAURANT (1969)

Direction: Arthur Penn
Screenplay: Arthur Penn and Venable Herndon
Photography: Michael Nebbia

In their reviews of Arthur Penn's *Alice's Restaurant*, Richard Schickel expressed the wish that it had "a slightly firmer spine"[1] and Moira Walsh lamented its "awkward, rather diffuse structure."[2] Although the road is once again and very obviously present, Arthur Penn has carefully and artfully constructed a network of visual images related to the road that together constitute the "spine," such as it is, of our recent American (subcultural) quest for a new form of community: vehicles, the church and its door, and faces. Form, these critics failed to observe, usually dictates meaning.

The road that takes folksinger Arlo Guthrie (playing himself) from the draft board to the Montana college and back to New York, that brings him to Stockbridge and back to his father in the hospital, that physically supports his hassle with the law, and finally that draws him away from Trinity Church is the substance of his life—a personal search for meaning, the quest of his own "thing." His comments to his father, Woody, and to his Oriental girl friend (Tina Chen) support what we see to be the case. There is no positive side to his self-understanding. After he has successfully failed his Army physical, he tells Woody: "The good things in my life always seem to come from not doing what I don't want to do. When they're not after me to do what I don't want to do—what do I want to do?" And to his girl friend he says: "I feel in a hurry to know what my thing is going to be." So in the end he pushes on—the road and his bus the symbols of his quest. The commodious Volkswagen bus, which always has room for others, suggests the open-hearted communal way that Arlo will pursue his thing.

For Arlo, then, the road like his bus is an open symbol. But for Ray Brock (James Broderick) and Shelly (Michael McClan-

61

athan), it is closed. They have formed the Trinity Racing Association; their motorcycles and the course they ride are confirmations of the cyclic patterns of their lives. Addicted to dope, Shelly is in and out of hospitals, up and down psychologically depending on the availability of a fix. The only way that he can break out of the enclosed pattern of his agony is by reaching into the very heart of his darkness, and so he rides headlong and alone into the empty night of death. Ironically, his only apparent victory is the loss of his life. Ray is hemmed in by the very cyclic pattern of his vision. When he moves from one place to another, it is in the quixotic hope that the new place will at last provide a way of living together that no one will want to "split" from. So at the end of the film when he proposes moving to Vermont to buy some land there, it is to achieve once and for all the utopia that failed at Trinity Church. Not only is his dream impossible, his own ineptitude is his unbeatable foe. The ostentatious symbol of his idealism is a Flower Car, retired significantly from funeral service.

A second key image, and certainly the most important to Penn's social statement, is the church, an "old wineskin" that Ray and Alice Brock (Pat Quinn) buy to keep their "new wine" in. "A place to be the way we want to be," Ray announces to Alice and Arlo as they take possession of the deconsecrated edifice. Almost as if they are playing out their respective parts in a religious ritual, Arlo intones "Amazing Grace!" in response to Ray's announcement. Yet whether we are hearing the words of this old hymn while watching a staged cure at the roadside revival or during a quiet moment at the end of the Housatonic Thanksgiving dinner, the words never really ring true on any level: "Amazing grace, / How sweet the sound / That saved a wretch like me; / I once was lost but now I'm found, / Was blind but now I see." For Arlo the church is simply a place to meet his friends, a way station in his quest for identity where he can achieve a momentary "high" in the fellowship of song and love.

It means far more, of course, to the Brocks. The simple though lovely old Stockbridge church is the ironic embodiment of an unspecified dream, their open experiment in communal existence. The film prompted Harvey Cox to offer this psychedelic reflection on our most recent variation on that perennial American effort made famous originally by the nineteenth-century Brook Farm experience: "Impaled between high-rise bureaucracies and nuclear families with 3.2 children, we feverishly scan the scene for something that will provide us with the family's warmth without its constriction, the city's freedom without its terrifying impersonality."[3]

It is Ray who will make persistent efforts to maintain the utopian "high" symbolized for him by his newly acquired home, his "heavenly city," whether remodeling it or coaxing Alice back to it for the Thanksgiving dinner with the promise that "it won't be like before." After Shelly's funeral, when Alice suggests that perhaps their "beauty" had not gotten through to Shelly, Ray answers: "Maybe we haven't been too beautiful lately." It is a rare moment of self-knowledge for Ray; he immediately proposes that they remarry as an instant return to beauty. As the wedding scene winds down, Ray frantically attempts to sustain their factitious beatitude.

Alice certainly shares most of Ray's hopes for the church. She has, however, firmer knowledge of her own limitations. She confides to Arlo, "I guess I'm the bitch had too many pups, couldn't take 'em all milking me." Alice tries the hardest to provide the right kind of atmosphere; yet despite her best efforts, her own deep need for love and affection keeps "crowding the pups out."

How effective a "grace" the church has been, how much it has helped them to see, becomes apparent through the visual meanings assigned to its door. The main entrance to the church is used visually in several ways: as an opening through which light shines, as a passageway, but most significantly as an arch framing the occupants. The door of the church appears several times in the film as a narrow source of light in the midst of darkness. Initially, the film cuts from the rather even obscurity of the New York club were Arlo is entertaining to the pervasive darkness outside the church, with a narrow stream of light coming from inside the church. After cutting inside where Ray supervises the redecoration of his "soul ship," the film jump-cuts to the darkness outside where later a single bulb is being screwed into a socket above the door, an added source of light that makes no appreciable dent in the darkness. Ray's "Let there be light" is an ironical commentary on their failure to be a light either for themselves or for others. The extreme upward tilt of the camera emphasizes the impossibility of their pretensions, by exaggerating the distance between ground and light. When Shelly is crowded out of the church, Alice runs through the dim light of the door into the ominous haze of night. Their experiment has done little to dispel the darkness.

As exit, of course, the door is the necessary passage to freedom from the constriction of the pseudofamily. Yet, although the door is most frequently and significantly shown as an exit from the church, one of the most interesting shots is of the arrival of the guests for the Thanksgiving dinner. Ray and Shelly ride their motorcycles up the outside ramp; and a floor-level camera, no doubt with the aid of some trick photography, catches them sailing through the door into the church. They have indeed threaded the eye of a needle in an absurdly risky display of virtuosity, but they have hardly entered into their kingdom.

Most meaningfully though, during both of the celebrations in the church—on Thanksgiving and during the wedding—we have decisive shots of the group framed in the arch of the door, a shot obviously made from the vestibule of the church. Enclosed in darkness, the group seems huddled together—a protection no doubt against the darkness, yet obviously also a statement about their loss of freedom, about the way Alice and Ray have crowded them in.

It is Penn's "haunting affection for the American face,"[4] however, mentioned by Penelope Gilliatt, that captures perfectly our potential for humor and capacity for suffering. The frame of Arlo's wry smile stands in marked contrast to the pathetic twitch on Shelly's face. The joy and expectation on the faces of Ray and Alice as they wait to take possession of the church is offset by the loneliness, almost emptiness, of Alice's face during the film's final, slow dolly shot that reveals there something between hope and despair, perhaps what Hawthorne described so brilliantly in "The Maypole of Merry Mount" as the fate of our countrymen—"care, and sorrow, and troubled joy."[5] The light during the final sequence is extremely important. Ray tries in vain to prevail upon Arlo to remain. "We'd all be some kind of family," he insists. As Ray goes in defeat back into the church, the light that was casting his shadow from a source to the left (the setting sun?) dims to near darkness. But as Arlo's voice is heard singing "Alice's Restaurant," the light rises on Alice from the right—not brilliantly, but nonetheless brightly, a light that somehow prevents her assimilation by the sterile whiteness of the church's façade, just as she had not experienced complete defeat within.

Throughout, the film's gentle visual irony supports Penn's variation on our "troubled joy." We see a drill team performing maneuvers on a field before the cut to the office where the dean of students at the Montana college informs the badly bruised Arlo that "American education has always been characterized by freedom of thought and expression." The accepted long hair of the revivalist contrasts wonderfully with the disgust of the truck driver when Arlo lets his hair down. In his newly acquired Microbus Arlo journeys to Stockbridge, passing patiently but hurriedly the individual trucks of an Army convoy that is holding up traffic. We hear Pete Seeger sing "Pastures of Plenty" for the dying Woody Guthrie, while we watch Woody's tortured breathing and see the strange weathered beauty of Seeger's mottled face. The second race that Ray and Shelly participate in, the one "in honor of the boys in Veet Naam [sic]," quickly ends for us in a cloud of dust and confusion. Shelly hides his heroin in a mobile, kept in the church; he hangs another mobile in the restaurant. The graceful balance of a mobile is something terribly foreign to Shelly, yet his life does hang by a thread. One of the most beautiful yet poignant scenes shows the rite of Shelly's burial. A traveling shot, apparently down a road bordering the cemetery, reveals the expanse of the gathering—Shelly's friends who brave the snow to throw flowers on his coffin. But they are spread out over the hillside; a succession of full shots emphasizes their isolation as Joni Mitchell sings "Songs to Aging Children."

One wonders, too, whether Arlo's Thanksgiving gift of the

donkey to Alice and Ray is no more than a mere setup for the draft-dodging latter-day-pilgrim's concern about how he is going "to get his ass across the border." No longer does the church bell announce the beginning of religious services; the "lord and lady of the manor," however, do announce by bell the completion of their love. There is a wry juxtaposition of the bell tolling after the Thanksgiving dinner and the knowing smiles on the faces of Arlo and Roger as they leave to dump the garbage. And after the wedding Ray's efforts to keep the fellowship together are commented on visually by a cut to the empty church and the descending balloons. Thus, aside from the "massacree" itself—Arlo's arrest by Officer Obie and the subsequent trial— there is sufficient visual irony for us to discern at least the "firm spine" of a prevailing mood in the film.

Ralph Ellison has described the "blues" as "an impulse to keep the painful details and episodes of a brutal experience alive in one's aching consciousness, to finger its jagged grain and to transcend it, not by the consolation of philosophy but by squeezing from it a near-tragic, near-cosmic lyricism."[6] Arlo Guthrie's "Alice's Restaurant Massacree" stands perhaps to the blues described by Ellison in much the same way as black humor today is related to the serious apocalyptic fiction of Hawthorne, Melville, and Poe. Rather than personal catastrophe expressed lyrically, we have lyric expression given to individual and corporate insanity. In the final analysis, *Alice's Restaurant* cannot be completely understood apart from its aural component, this talking-blues song, which in expanded form becomes the background and counterpoint for Penn's visual odyssey. The alternating moods of serenity and excitement, of calm and movement carry us through to the pointed synchronisation of Arlo's commercial and the last shot of Alice frozen and alone on the steps of the church. Alice is one who needs more than she can give. You may not be able to get anything that you want at Alice's restaurant, but you can surely get Alice—if you are lucky enough to be one of her pups. Yet what do you have when you get Alice? Alice is the problem, not the solution to the search for new ways of living together.

Alice's Restaurant has apparently as firm a visual spine as the contemporary quest for meaning can, in Penn's estimate, support. It is a gentle apocalypse, a visually lyrical celebration of the crisis of our times when, convinced of the failure of old communal forms, we face the inadequacy of the new.

THE LAST PICTURE SHOW (1971)

Direction: Peter Bogdanovich
Screenplay: Larry McMurtry and Peter Bogdanovich (from the novel by McMurtry)
Photography: Robert Surtees

The Last Picture Show was received with such universal approval by the critics that it could easily have been "the first picture show" of a new era. Appearing toward the end of a fairly typical recent film year (dreary by any standards), it was called everything from a "lovely film" (Vincent Canby) to "superb" (Hollis Alpert) to "the most impressive work by a young American director since *Citizen Kane*" (Paul D. Zimmerman).[7] *Film Facts*, published by the American Film Institute, almost self-consciously registered the tally of major critical response as "14 favorable, 2 mixed, 0 negative."[8] Peter Bogdanovich gambled with black-white photography, unfamiliar faces in important roles, and a classical style of film narration borrowed from John Ford and Howard Hawks (though not offensively derivative), and his gamble paid off admirably.

The film is set in a small, desolate Texas town named Anarene in 1951-52 (the location scenes were filmed in Archer City, Texas, novelist McMurtry's home town). There is a definite air of nostalgia in the treatment of historical references, and this was scarcely missed by the critics, many of whom were happy to note its authenticity of tone because it was the period of their youth that the film was reviewing. Yet for all this there is a freshness to Bogdanovich's handling of McMurtry's semi-autobiographical material that makes the film a major American contribution to the genre of film journey.

The Last Picture Show is not just another version of the agonies of growth out of adolescence in a small town environment. Bogdanovich was quoted as having said, "Small town life in America isn't like *Our Town*." There is, however, a deeper affinity between his film and Thornton Wilder's classic play than he apparently realized. On the visual level alone, they could not, obviously, be farther apart. Yet certain major themes are held in common. Both works view life with varying degrees of regret, *Our Town* because of man's inability to realize life's full potential as he lives it, *The Last Picture Show* because life seems to offer so little in the way of opportunity. Insofar as they address themselves to nostalgia's richest sense as the "remembrance of things past," the works are also similar in theme. Emily's attempt to relive the day of her twelfth birthday leads only to the frustrating though humbling realization that all human experience is transitory. The thematic prominence Bogdanovich has given the Hank Williams song "Why Don't You Love Me" suggests more than mere musical reminiscence. The film's realistic evocation of a dreary past undercuts perfectly love's romanticized memory in Williams's lyrics: "Why don't you love me like you used to do / How come you treat me like a worn-out shoe . . . ?"

What makes Anarene's class of '51 different from others is signaled in the film by the closing of the Royal Theatre, the town's movie house. It is the end of an era, and Anarene, like so many American way stations on the road West, is a dying town. With television bringing the perennial American illusion right into each living room ("Strike it Rich" is on in one glimpse of the tube), cinema's local shrine must close for lack of patronage. (The films shown provide ironic commentary on the reality of Anarene: *Father of the Bride*, with its idealized family stability, and the last picture show itself, *Red River*, in which John Wayne's call to start the cattle drive highlights the glamor of a Western about beginnings in a western town near the end.) The theatre had been the center of the town's social life; the pool hall and the café were second best. The church, sadly enough, is nowhere in evidence. The dissolution of Anarene's "ties that bind" typifies on a deeper level the general rupture of America's social fabric at midcentury caused by television's almost universal availability and unfortunate popularity.

Sonny Crawford (Timothy Bottoms) and Duane Jackson (Jeff Bridges), seniors of the class of '51, when not serving as co-captains of the worst football team in the school's history, spend most of their time at one of the three public places owned by Sam the Lion (Ben Johnson), a former cowboy, now apparently the sole father figure to Anarene's youth. From the home base of pool hall, café and movie theatre, their forays into life appear as so many abortive sexual excursions. Sonny goes from limited petting with Charlene Duggs (Sharon Taggart) in the back of the picture show and the front of his pickup truck, to a painful, though maturing experiment in sex with Ruth Popper (Cloris Leachman), the wife of his coach, then to a quickly annulled (unconsummated) marriage with the local tease Jacy Farrow (Cybill Shepherd), and finally to near seduction by Jacy's mother, Lois (Ellen Burstyn). The pattern of sexual liaison—abortive, interrupted, inconclusive, abandoned—becomes a metaphoric comment on man's frantic attempt to reach for solid moorings in the chaos of disintegrating structures.

Jacy begins the senior year as Duane's girl friend, but at her mother's condescending suggestion that she would never be satisfied with a poor husband, she breaks into the fast company of rich friends from Wichita Falls, but discovers at a nude swimming party there that the wealthy Bobby Sheen (Gary Brockette) will not take her as a virgin. With perfect cunning, she allows Duane, after one missed cue, to deflower her in a motel room, while a chorus of classmates sits approvingly in parked cars outside. Ready now for Bobby, she discards Duane, only to be jilted herself when Bobby marries another girl. Like an injured tigress fighting back, she permits her mother's lover, Abilene (Clu Gulager), to seduce her, then takes Sonny from Ruth while Duane is away working in the oil fields. The boys quarrel and fight; Sonny is seriously hurt by a savage blow from a broken beer bottle. Jacy's restless flirtation threatens the very foundation of the boys' friendship; she is well on her way toward exceeding the disruptive contacts of her mother's earlier odyssey, with little hope that she will ever gain the latter's insight into the limits of sex.

The film follows the novel on which it is based (McMurtry collaborated with Bogdanovich on the script) very closely, almost slavishly. There are however a few changes that are less minor than they appear on the surface. Of the influential critics, two who had read the novel—Pauline Kael and Andrew Sarris[9] —implied that certain omissions were either in good taste or an

attempt to romanticize the material. The episode of sexual initiation is mercifully limited to the humorous encounter between
the mute boy Billy (Sam Bottoms) and the town's grotesque
whore Jimmie Sue, an event that is preceded in the novel by
group commerce with a blind heifer (Sonny and Billy abstain-
ing). In the novel Lois Farrow seduces Sonny, an opportunity
that is offered in the film, yet refused—for good reason. The
novel in general is less restrained in its instances of sexual contact (although it is certainly never offensive); in fact, the meaning and place of sex in man's growth to maturity would seem to
be its principal theme. The wisdom that Sam the Lion imparts
to Lois deals primarily with the value of sex. "I think he was
the only man in that whole horny town who knew what sex was
worth," she tells Sonny. "I probably never would have learned
myself if it hadn't been for Sam."[10] Later in the same conversation, she explains the basis of their love:

> It's terrible to only find one man your whole life who
> knows what it's worth, Sonny. It's just terrible. I
> wouldn't be tellin' you if it wasn't. I've looked too—
> you wouldn't bu-lieve how I've looked. When Sam,
> when Sam . . . the Lion was seventy years old he
> could just walk in . . . I don't know, hug me and call
> me Lois or something an' do more for me than any-
> body. *He* really knew what *I* was worth, an' the rest of
> them haven't, not one man in the whole
> country. . . .[11]

The film's version of the same conversation omits mention of
sex; although Lois's gratitude seems far less specific, it is nonetheless clear that she is indebted to Sam alone. She says wistful-
ly: "If it hadn't been for him I would have missed it, whatever it
is."

In Anarene sex separates rather than unites because there
are no longer any shared bases for communion, only the rubble
of decaying forms. To emphasize the trauma of growth in a rap-
idly deteriorating environment and the desperate need to absorb
the lessons of dignity while their sources last, death marks the
film's middle and its end. Sam the Lion dies suddenly from a

stroke while Sonny and Duane are on a wild jaunt into Mex-ico.[12] They return to discover that he has left his possessions to those whose work or interest helped sustain them: the pool hall to Sonny; the café to its waitress Genevieve (Eileen Brennan), whose elemental sense of justice and maternal concern reflect her close association with Sam; the theatre to Miss Mosey, who had sold candy and popcorn in its lobby for as long as anyone could remember. At the film's end, with Jacy away at college and Duane leaving for military service in Korea, Sonny must accept the tragic death of his young friend Billy whom he had learned truly to care for and protect after his earlier thoughtless complicity in the boy's sexual initiation. Sam's rebuke at the time, accepted by Sonny, undoubtedly launched his ascent to manhood.

The technical device that Bogdanovich uses to frame his film gives it, in the final analysis, more than visual neatness. It elevates the theatre to the level of symbol. The film begins with the still functioning movie house in center frame, then the cam-era pans up the desolate, windy main street into the heart of Anarene's story. The final pan back down the deserted highway that has just unnecessarily claimed Billy's life is superimposed on Sonny's muted reconciliation with Ruth Popper. They sit in the strained atmosphere of her kitchen, self-effacing and re-morseful, holding hands unemotionally across the top of the table; as Ruth absolves Sonny with a tentative "Never you mind, honey, never you mind," the scene dissolves slowly into the closing shot of the main street and its abandoned movie house. The film begins and ends with road and theatre. The lat-ter like the community it symbolizes is dead; the former, ever-present and enduring, either takes life (Billy) or is used by those who are going nowhere (Jacy and Duane). Sonny and Ruth, no longer sexual objects to each other, but not yet personal subjects of friendship's mature bond, are all that remain of the buried past.

Richard Schickel, stressing his contemporaneity with the film's youth and for this reason inclined perhaps to interpret it too narrowly as "some lessons in growing up," nevertheless expressed more clearly than any the hope exemplified by contact with "an extended family" (the boy's real parents are scarcely mentioned): "The way out of an adolescence that always carries with it the threat of becoming perpetual is through decent connections with those few adults who, whatever their other problems, have at least made this journey successfully and are willing to show and tell what it's like."[13] The film's viewpoint may actually be more urgent; namely, that it is *only* through the challenge of wisdom gained through honest suffering that any hope at all remains for the successful nurture of youth. Schickel continues: "The movie says what we all know—that too few adults are willing to perform these vital initiatory functions—but it adds a point that, in our present romanticizing of rebellious youth, we often forget, that a youth has to reach out to them, make known in some civil way his pain and need."[14] Schickel may possibly be rendering far more explicit a process that is of its nature indirect, however necessary; he has also, I have implied, minimized the potentially catastrophic effect of that sense of "loss of world" experienced between the passing of one era and the establishment of the next.

EASY RIDER (1969)

Direction: Dennis Hopper
Screenplay: Peter Fonda, Dennis Hopper, and Terry Southern
Photography: Laszlo Kovacs

According to Peter Fonda, "easy rider" is a Southern expression "for a whore's old man, not a pimp, but the dude who lives with a chick. Because he's got the easy ride. Well, that's what's happened to America, man. Liberty's become a whore, and we're all taking an easy ride."[15] He includes in this indictment the two heroes of the film, Wyatt and Billy, and claims to be put out by all those people, critics included, who come away from the film thinking that Wyatt and Billy were meant to be "free souls." What we have here is that all too common gap between intention and realization. Wyatt and Billy are certainly *not* free, but the film is weighted in such a way that it seems that they are *meant* to be. The ending of the film, in which they are the victims of evil, carries much more weight than the beginning of the film, in which they are the doers of evil (with consequences that are never adverted to). Furthermore, on the one occasion when the idea of freedom is expressly discussed, they are the ones who are made out to be the true representatives of freedom. This judgment is rendered by a third character named George, whose role is that of the fool who speaks wisdom, right after the three of them have been forced to leave a restaurant because of the hostility of the other diners:

GEORGE: What you represent to them is freedom.
BILLY: What the hell's wrong with freedom, man. That's what it's all about.
GEORGE: Oh, yeah; that's right—that's what it's all about, all right. But talking about it and being it— that's two different things. . . . 'Course don't ever tell anybody that they're not free, cause then they're gonna get real busy killin' and maimin' to prove to you that they are. Oh, yeah—they're gonna talk to you, and talk to you, and talk to you about individ-

74

ual freedom—but they see a free individual, it's
gonna scare 'em.

What they see is Wyatt and Billy.

The characters of Wyatt (Peter Fonda) and Billy (Dennis
Hopper) are apparently named for the Western heroes Wyatt
Earp and Buffalo Bill. As one critic observes, the two probably
represent a total of one person: Billy is the id and animal part;
Wyatt the ego and soul. "It is not at all curious, then, that they
don't communicate overtly with each other, except in cases
where the body (Hopper) says to the mind (Fonda), let's move
on, I'm aching, and the mind says, well, OK."[16] On an allegorical level, this mind/body sets out on a journey to rediscover
America, moving from West to East, as if to find out what was
so manifest about that destiny that made the first settlers move
from East to West. Wyatt's helmet and jacket, decorated with
the stars and stripes, prompt Billy to refer to him once as Captain America; and near the end of their journey, when Wyatt
says to Billy, "We blew it," he is speaking both literally and al-
legorically. But on neither level are the circumstances of their
"blowing it" ever made clear.

When did they "blow it"? The answer may well be "at the
beginning." We first meet them playing the middleman in a
Mexican dope deal, buying and selling cocaine in order to finance their trip. This is their original sin, so to speak. No comment is made on the morality of the act, unless it be in the song
that plays over it ("The pusher don't care how if you live or if
you die. God damn the pusher"). But neither this song nor any
of the others come through with the authority of Alan Price's
songs in *O Lucky Man!*; they are always something less than a
rock variation of the classical chorus. Having made their wad,
Wyatt and Billy hop on their motorcycles and off they go—like
modern centaurs, a combination of man and machine.[17]

Where are they going? First of all, to the Mardi Gras in
New Orleans, and then to Florida (from which Billy, like Ratso
in *Midnight Cowboy*, expects some kind of salvation; but as
John Simon remarks, what makes sense in a dying denizen of
the Bronx slums is incomprehensible in a Californian[18]). A good

three-fourths of the film, however, is taken up with various encounters along the way. There is the land itself: America, seen through Laszlo Kovacs's expert lens, is still beautiful in its mountains and valleys and rivers and plains. It is still beautiful in some of its people. Wyatt and Billy share a meal alfresco with a plainspoken rancher who has as many children as Christ had apostles ("My wife's Catholic," he explains). Wyatt congratulates him: "It's not every man that can live off the land, you know. You do your own thing in your own time. You should be proud." But this sort of thing is not for him. He and Billy push on, while "Wasn't Born to Follow" plays on the soundtrack.

They pick up a hitch-hiker who turns out to be the leader of a commune of hippies. Again, it is a meal that becomes the symbol of community: While grace is said ("Thank you for a place to make a stand"), the camera pans in a full circle with the simple intent of showing us the faces of an America still looking to the future. Will they make it? Wyatt says yes. Why not stay then and make a stand? Not Billy: "I gotta get out of here, man." As for Wyatt: Well, it's true that time's running out and he's hip about time (that was why he threw his watch away at the start of the trip), but *he* can't stay either, he's just gotta go.

At this point they meet George Hanson. Passing through New Mexico, they get caught up in a parade, get arrested for parading without a permit, and end up in a cell adjoining the one in which George Hanson (Jack Nicholson) is just coming out of a long drunk. He turns out to be a small-town lawyer who has done a lot of work for the A.C.L.U. but who has become something of a regular at the city jail because of his affinity to alcohol. His dad is obviously a big shot in town and he himself so goodnatured that the Sheriff can only admonish him and let him go. With little more than a smile George manages to get Wyatt and Billy off the hook, and on impulse decides to go along with them to the Mardi Gras.

He never makes it. In one of the more dramatically effective scenes of the film, Wyatt, Billy and George stop off at a restaurant in a Southern town but are forced to leave when the remarks of the local customers fill the air with hostility. Hopper the director describes his method in this and similar scenes: "I wanted to use actual residents of the towns we went into, and let them say pretty much what they would actually say when they saw our long hair and so on. I'd outline what I wanted in a scene, give them a few specific lines, and let them improvise from there."[19] That night, at a campsite outside the town, reflecting upon their experience, the three travelers have that talk about freedom and then go to sleep. A pair of legs moves into view, a hand comes down with a stick on somebody's head; all at once several men converge on the three sleeping bags, with arms swinging. When the attack is over, George Hanson lies dead.

A *Kyrie Eleison* broods over his death and brings the two survivors into the moldy atmosphere of a New Orleans whorehouse with religious paintings on the wall and sayings about God and man's mortality. Wyatt and Billy, apparently still looking for America, dive into Mardi Gras with two of the whores. But Death draws them into a cemetery and into the world of LSD. There among the tombs, with stone angels looking on, they descend into a hellish brew of sex, death and religion. The Christian Creed bubbles from the lips of one of the whores, while declarations of love and hate spurt out of some murky hollow in Wyatt's soul—love and hate for a mother who left him because she was such a fool. We must suppose that, on the literal level, Wyatt had a mother; on the allegorical level she is, of course, America.

This mother has betrayed us. Even though we were good little children, she has left us. Even though we were innocent, she has abandoned us to our deaths—the death of our dreams, the death of ourselves. Wyatt has premonitions of his death, apparently on both the literal and allegorical levels: "I think I'm going to crash," he says, and once in a flash-forward he glimpses his own death (and Billy's) in a burst of fire on the highway. But what Wyatt never articulates (except perhaps in the cryptic "We blew it") is the connection between their deaths and their so-called innocence.

They are killed on the highway by two rednecks because, if

we are to believe George Hanson, they represent freedom. But what do Billy and Wyatt know about freedom? Freedom, to them, is the throwing over of every responsibility, every relationship, every commitment, every obligation, every boundary. Without boundaries, their search is doomed from the very start. But this is the theme that *Easy Rider* never truly explores (even if intended). "All I wanted was to be free, and that's the way it turned out to be." The irony of this sentiment, expressed in the last song we hear, does not extend dramatically to the sad fact that they never really knew what they wanted.

MIDNIGHT COWBOY (1969)

Direction: John Schlesinger
Screenplay: Waldo Salt (from the novel by James Leo Herlihy)
Photography: Adam Holender

Though *Midnight Cowboy*, like the novel it is based on, can be and has been read as an exposé of the hazards of man's personal quest for meaning in the midst of the impersonal city, John Schlesinger's ...m leans for a variety of reasons toward the sphere of the social. As a tribute to the power of fraternal love, *Midnight Cowboy* is superficially like *Scarecrow*; the narrative thread of each traces the development of the bond of friendship between contemporary loners up to the moment of self-sacrificing love. Herlihy's novel is divided into three parts, the first of which explores Joe Buck's life prior to his departure for New York, while the latter two cover the material of the film's narrative. The novel is of course Joe's story whereas the film quickly makes Ratso Rizzo a major focus of individual attention. The material of the first two-fifths of the novel—Joe's background —is compressed into a few brief, inconclusive flashbacks; and only a hint or two is offered of Ratso's personal history.[20]

What comes to the fore in Waldo Salt's adaptation of the novel—under Schlesinger's direction—is an obsession for the details of the American way of life, the countryside and the city. In a devastating juxtaposition of sight and sound the film begins on a note of caustic commentary. We hear pistol shots and hoofs before we see anything but a blank white screen as the camera pulls away to reveal the bare screen of an empty small-town drive-in theatre. A child's hobby—horse rocks back and forth in the playground under the screen; there are real horses grazing in the pasture beyond. The Western has replaced the West, or at least they endure together without meaning. While the song "Everybody's Talkin' " swells to dominate the sound track, the camera cuts to Joe Buck (Jon Voight) in a shower

79

preparing to leave home. It angles up his body giving us a full side view of the glistening object he will shortly offer for sale. (The only part of it he can later sell with any assurance is its blood.) On the road from Texas to New York, the "Jesus Saves" sign is simply another detail in the patchwork of cultural signals along with the more thematically humorous "The World's Longest Hotdog." El Dorado is reduced from continental symbol of promise to mere sign; it is the name of a cheap roadside motel. The flashing acronym of Mutual of New York seems to dominate the Manhattan skyline; Joe is of course illiterate enough to think the object of his quest is spelled MONY.

Joe's radio is his inseparable companion; it is his transistorized umbilical cord to the superficialities of society. His passage East over the American countryside is marked by a quick succession of day and night shots—different towns, other stations. The radio announces his arrival in New York. A street interviewer asks women their "idea of a man"; the random responses—"Gary Cooper," "someone who can talk in bed," "someone not afraid of sex"—intensify his naive anticipation of the availability of his prey. The television set in his hotel room will not work, he is dumbfounded to discover, unless he feeds it a quarter. In the city Joe will of course pay and pay again for his addiction to the illusions of the media until the symbolic moment of passage when he must pawn his radio in order to eat.

The media that had poisoned Joe's ambition inevitably comment on the absurdity of his sexual odyssey. As he tussles with the Park Avenue hooker atop the TV remote control, the set responds successively with a prehistoric beast lunging through the forest, a bishop preaching against the death of God, and Al Jolson in black face. Creamed corn in a bowl and a spray of coins from a slot machine register self-consciously the moment of climax. A movie-house homosexual experience has the launching of a rocket as its cinematic foreground. The television talk show that Joe finds absorbing features an inane discussion of cosmetics for the poodles of lonely people.

As he cruises down a crowded Manhattan street for the first time, the rapid cuts deliver the city's only visual message:

sex and money. A dated knight in hustler's armor—boots and a cowboy jacket with fringes—Joe follows one woman, then another: cut to a jewelry store, close-up of a large gem. Joe pursues another potential victim: cut to an open vault seen through the bank window. Though Schlesinger's sexual imagery is less than subtle, his association of sex and money is clearly persistent.

If Joe's ambition is wealth through sexual conquest, it is his fortuitous encounter with Ratso Rizzo (Dustin Hoffman) that introduces money, pure and simple, as an object of the American quest, lately from dire need. Baptized Enrico Salvatore Rizzo, Ratso, despising his seemingly appropriate nickname and wanting to be called Rico, is a small-time urban variation of the con man who has forever roamed our literary landscape. By contrast with Joe's attractive though presumptuous packaging, Ratso's consumptive body is deformed and his beard is perpetual stubble. Still he uses his body for all the sympathy it can get—the way of the confidence man. Ratso is reduced to living off of country mice like Joe; change left in telephone coin slots typifies his level of achievement. Joe must eventually share Ratso's dismal "pad" in an abandoned tenement house.

Although their personalities emerge in the encounter of mutual need, we never really know enough of their individual histories to be satisfied with any explanation of their present condition other than social victimization. In brief flashbacks (Joe's fantasies are about the past), we are teased with hints of inadequate attention from a vagrant grandmother (Ruth White) and a traumatic relationship with Crazy Annie, a town whore. Ratso alludes to a Catholic upbringing and confessional scruples, and laments his father's early death as a subway bootblack; they even visit the cemetery plot where Ratso's characteristic gesture is to steal artificial flowers for his father from another grave. When Ratso dreams it is about the future; he imagines himself controlling the wealth of the golden-age darlings of Miami Beach as poolside pimp organizing Joe's services. Even in his dreams, he is routed. What Ratso needs more than anything is the healing warmth of the southern sun. Sunshine and coconut milk, both presumably free, are sufficient to sustain life, he informs Joe. All that the city provides their likes against the onslaught of a northern winter is a useless sun of gold and white light bulbs.

Specific camera techniques confirm the primacy of the city. The use of the zoom lens to identify important details or to discover Joe in the river of humanity flooding the New York sidewalks leaves the viewer with the impression that the city depersonalizes; at any rate, we repeatedly see the whole before the part, the masses before the individual, the feet before the man. A device with similar effect that Schlesinger uses is the oblique introduction of his subject matter. The camera glides down a crowded bar until it reaches Joe. The person next to him is not an extra; we are seeing Ratso for the first time. A close shot follows a tray with two drinks to a sidewalk table just as Joe and Ratso pass; Ratso impresses Joe by appearing to know the supposed hustler sitting with an older woman.

Even Joe's sexual encounters, although revealing his ineptitude as a stud, his delusions of adequacy, seem more aptly designed as an overview of the types of urban perversion. Cass (Sylvia Miles), the Park Avenue hooker-with-poodle, who fields Joe's amateurish request for directions to the Statue of Liberty with the brilliant "It's up in Central Park taking a leak" (giving us some indication of the sophisticated odds against him), is an accomplished confidence woman herself who must be paid rather than pay. Mr. O'Daniel (John McGiver), who Ratso claims will organize Joe's efforts, is not the expected super-pimp but a religious fanatic urging Jesus as the cure for lonesomeness before his blinking statue of the Sacred Heart. In a short-order café Joe's chance boothmate is a young fetishist who runs a rubber rat over her own and her brother's head. Reduced to homosexual encounters in 42nd Street movie houses, Joe is tricked into allowing free fellatio to a penniless schoolboy. The shy career girl (Brenda Vaccaro), at the Warhol-clan party, who sweetly tolerates Joe's early inability to perform, becomes a beast of a bed partner (triumphal music accompanies their frenzied coupling) with needy friends also willing to pay. Completing a spectrum of psychological types,

Towny (Barnard Hughes), the elderly businessman from Chicago, is a homosexual masochist who misses his mother.

The only genuine relationship that the film offers is the one that grows slowly but surely between Joe and Ratso. The irony that the film adds to the novel is to compound the sacrifice Joe must make in order to take his friend South—by suggesting his "arrival" as a successful stud. It is precisely at the mod party where Joe meets Sylvia, who calls a friend in order to share him, that Ratso collapses. Their bond though is too strong for a slow harvest of success. Joe extorts sufficient cash from the aging homosexual and the two immediately begin their urgent flight South. Touching imagery of rebirth confirms the transforming power of their love and the sacrifice it has prompted. Joe finally calls Ratso "Rico" as he has wanted all along. He discards his midnight outfit and buys them both new shirts that herald the sun of a new day. Rico's is the last with brightly painted palm trees on it. Joe's plain shirt suggests the dawn of a more realistic expectation from life; Rico's is a comforting shroud for his passage through death.

Although Stanley Kauffmann's observation that the film "simply states that, at any social level, the exchange of trust and devotion is the only sure spiritual oasis"[21] may itself be an adequate indication of its preoccupation with the contemporary American cultural climate, Jan Dawson in *Sight and Sound* offers a more precise assessment of the film's emphasis: "British director John Schlesinger's first American feature confines itself to the now familiar terrain of the American Dream turned nightmare; a society so obsessed with material prosperity that its citizens—equating sex, love and money—add themselves to the unending stream of desirable consumer goods and suffer from the concomitant problems of advertising, fashionable packaging and rapid obsolescence."[22]

As the film begins so it ends—with an impression of the impersonal city. The early sequence that follows Joe's introduction to the streets of New York shows an unconscious man stretched out on the sidewalk in front of Tiffany's! The passers-by ignore him; Joe comes into view, concerned, looking first at the man, then at the detached faces of the passing crowd. Confused, he too moves off, though slowly and with a backward glance. At the end, on the bus entering Miami, when Joe realizes that Ratso is dead, he informs the driver. The passengers do nothing but crane their necks to gawk at death. One woman, detached and oblivious, more concerned about the end of her trip than the presence of the enemy, continues to powder her nose. The final shot through the window of the bus frames a frightened Joe, embracing his peaceful friend; the window reflects the skyline of Miami. The spectre of the city's inhumanity remains. Harry Nilsson's voice returns with the ironic refrain of the film's thematic song: "I'm goin' where the sun keeps shinin' / Through the pourin' rain, / Goin' where the weather suits my clothes."

BALLAD OF A SOLDIER (1959)

Direction: Grigori Chukhrai
Screenplay: Valentin Yoshov and Grigori Chukhrai
Photography: Vladimir Nikolayev

Ballad of a Soldier opens and closes with the image of a road. It is the only road that leads in and out of a small farming community in Russia. A woman is looking down the length of the road. The narrator's voice informs us that she is looking for her son but will never see him come back because he died in the war. Weighted with this knowledge, we watch his story unfold. Like a ballad, it goes very quickly to the heart of the matter and to matters of the heart. And when our own hearts are most deeply stirred, we remember that he is dead.

Alyosha (Vladimir Ivashov) is a nineteen-year-old soldier serving in the early stages of the Second World War somewhere on the western front in Russia. Russia is still reeling from the German attack of June 1941. The war effort so far has cost her nearly twenty million dead, or one-tenth of her population. But the enemy is never seen, except in the opening sequence, and even then he is hidden behind the armor of a tank. "In this film," the director has said, "I wanted to speak to my comrades, men of my age who became soldiers as soon as they left school. I wanted to show what sort of man my hero was. Discarding battle scenes, I looked for a subject that would show war for what it is."[23] He succeeds in showing us what sort of man his hero is—a very good young man (for some viewers, unbelievably good), the salt of the earth, the hope of Russia. But Chukhrai's very success in this first aim is the partial cause of his failure in the second. We do not see war for what it is. We see something of its effects in the life of Alyosha and in the lives of the people around him, the hardships, the separations. But with one or two exceptions war speaks only to what is noble in this people; it awakens no evil in the heart.

Insofar as war intensifies and complicates life, it is used as a metaphor for what a youth must go through on his way to adulthood. As reward for an act of heroism, Alyosha is granted a six-day pass to return home and see his mother. Two days to get there, two to spend there, and two to get back—but it does not work out that way; people and things rise up and converge on him, and he cannot but respond. The ballad thus takes on a mythic dimension: There is no returning to the past (uncomplicated youth) if one is to remain faithful to the present (adult responsibility).

The opening sequence, in which Alyosha becomes a hero almost in spite of himself, is a revelation of hope as a deep inward resource without which the passage from youth to adulthood could never be made. Alyosha is serving on the front line as a signal corpsman when he and his companion are spotted by four enemy tanks. His companion flees, but he finds himself staying and radioing back the news. Then he runs for his life. The tanks pursue, relentlessly, inhumanly, as if his body were a magnet designed to be crushed by the terrible weight it draws upon itself. Through the camera's eye we see the tanks as he sees them in the wild fright of his mind, turning upside down and still in pursuit. He drops down exhausted in the open field and raises a thin rifle against the monstrous enemy. One tank explodes in flames, then another. The other two are routed. William F. Lynch describes the moment well: "A slow, halfbelieving grin begins to break out on the face of the boy. The belief in his heroism comes halfway out, as well as the dawning realization of hope."[24]

The rest of the film makes very clear that, important as it is, hope as a deep inward resource is not enough; it has to be supported from the outside. "Hope," says Lynch, "is truly on the inside of us, but hope is an interior sense that there is help on the outside of us."[25] On his difficult journey home help comes to Alyosha, or he gives help to others, in a series of personal encounters that take place in a society pushed to the extreme, when fears and longings are quick to surface. Chukhrai and Nikolayev, his director of photography, keep us very much aware of this larger social context by an alternation of long shots of the land and its people with tight close-ups of faces.

Alyosha's first encounter is with a troop of soldiers going in the opposite direction. When they find out he is going home, one of them asks him to take a present to his wife. What shall it be? Alyosha is on pins and needles to be off, but he finds himself waiting until they wrangle a bar of soap from the sergeant. At the train station he meets a crippled soldier (Eugeni Urbanski) who cannot bring himself to return to his wife in his present condition. Alyosha takes time to convince him that he is wrong, and as a result misses his train. When he leaps onto a passing freight, he enters upon the most significant of all his encounters.

A young girl, not suspecting his presence, climbs into the same car. When he comes out of hiding, she screams and tries to jump out but the train is already in motion. Pauline Kael, whose view of a film is always to be reckoned with, sees *Ballad of a Soldier* as a regression to nineteenth-century values and fusses at audiences for loving it. "It takes us back to the days when love was sweet and innocent" and "only people without principles thought about sex."[26] Actually, with Alyosha and the girl Shura (Shanna Prokhorenko), sex is very much on their minds. The girl's first thought is that the boy will rape her; and later, when they begin to trust each other, it is clear that the boy wants her badly but will not take advantage of her. It is not at all unbelievable that such males could be and be fully alive in the twentieth century. They existed in the forties, they exist now. Even Alyosha's repugnance for marital infidelity, which Miss Kael calls "priggish," is understandable. After all, when he brings the bar of soap as a present to the soldier's wife and finds out she is living with another man, he reacts, rightly or wrongly, somewhat as the husband would, having been sent in his name. Furthermore, Alyosha is still very young.

The time spent with the girl is time away from his mother. The war will force the mother to release her son in death, but it also precipitates the process whereby she must release him to another woman. Though Alyosha is still on his way to his mother, his heart is very much with Shura. People fall in and out of love, but no lover who has fallen "in" can ever imagine himself falling "out." C. S. Lewis comments: "The event of falling in love is of such a nature that we are right to reject as intolerable the idea that it should be transitory. In one high bound it has overleaped the massive wall of our selfhood; it has made appetite itself altruistic, tossed personal happiness aside as a triviality and planted the interests of another in the centre of our being."[27] And yet, though unaware of any intrinsic possibility of impermanency in their love for each other, Alyosha and Shura sense very deeply the state of impermanency in which the war has put them. The very train that brings them together takes them apart. Once, they are accidentally separated when Alyosha sets out for a bucket of water; and the train, with Shura asleep in one of its cars, goes off without him. To their great relief, they find each other again at the station of the town to which Shura was going. There, however, they must part without any sure hope that they will ever meet again. Alyosha continues on his journey to his mother, but his thoughts on the train are all with Shura. We see her image superimposed on the landscape that races by. Once he thinks he sees her on the train. Did he tell her he loved her? "Why didn't I tell her?" Frantically he makes a move to get off and go back.

But at last he finds himself on the road that will take him to his village. He has survived the bombardment of the troop train; he has come the rest of the way by foot and truck. How little time is left! His mother (Antonina Maximova) crosses into the fields without seeing him as the Army truck that picked him up carries him into the village. A neighbor, sighting him, rushes into the fields to get her. The mother drops what she is doing and races toward her son; he runs to meet her, and all our emotion runs with them. This is one of those archetypal images that Carl Jung talks about—a primordial image in the depths of the human psyche that allows an artist to speak not only with his own voice but with a thousand voices. Mother and son hardly have time for more than a kiss. "You've grown! Do you have to shave?" The horn blows. "I have to go. I'll come back, mother."

But actually Alyosha has already gone from her, though neither of them knows it, and he will never come down that road again. The intensity of war, having telescoped the passage of his life from youth to adulthood into a few short days, tears him from his mother's arms and hurls him, incredulous, into the arms of death. Unseen but felt throughout the film, this death marks not only the end of a life but the point of no return.

THE GODFATHER (1972)

Direction: Franci. Ford Coppola
Screenplay: Mario Puzo and Francis Ford Coppola (based on the novel by Puzo)
Photography: Gordon Willis

There are two metaphors of journey, one the reverse of the other, that interact in *The Godfather*. The waiting car is a sign of passage from life to death. Baptism, traditionally, is a sign of passage from death to life. Both are rituals, both intersect at the end of the film. A godfather orders a waiting car for all his enemies; while his orders are being carried out, he stands at his nephew's baptism. To the extent that the first ritual is made effective, the second is rendered meaningless.

The tension between life and death has its visual counterpart in the film: Some scenes are suffused with light, others steeped in varying shades of darkness. The former take us into a world that pulses with the rhythms of natural life, the latter into the labyrinthine ways of the underworld; the former into a garden of Eden, the latter into the surrounding wilderness. Coppola sets up the contrast with a masterful hand in the very first scene. While hundreds of guests gather in Don Vito's garden to celebrate his daughter's wedding, he himself holds court in a room overlooking the festivities. Outside, the wine flows freely; inside, the machine is carefully oiled—with a few judicious words or, if necessary, with blood.

Don Vito Corleone (Marlon Brando) is a man to whom anybody can come for help and not be disappointed, if only he is willing to show respect now and gratitude, upon request, later. One of Corleone's petitioners on this particular morning is an undertaker whose daughter has been injured in an attempted rape. He wants revenge, an eye for an eye. Actually, he wants more: He wants the death of the two assailants. Because he believed in America, he had first gone to the police. The two boys were arrested, brought to trial, and set free. Now he must come to Don Corleone for justice. Corleone rebukes him on

90

three counts: for not coming to him in the first place, for asking for more than an eye for an eye, and for having spurned the Don's friendship in the past. The first rebuke points up the illusion of the American dream. That dream, whatever it is, is not for Sicilians. There is no justice to be had from a judge who sells himself like the worst whore in the streets. If there were, the Godfather would never have come into being: He administers the justice that the courts refuse. The second rebuke stresses the fact that this justice is administered according to principle. One must not let oneself be carried away. The name of the game is equalizing vengeance.[28]

The third rebuke is meant to be the strongest. Such homage is the source of the Godfather's power. "We have known each other many years, you and I," he says to the undertaker, "but until this day you never came to me for counsel or help. I can't remember the last time you invited me to your house for coffee though my wife is godmother to your only child. Let us be frank. You spurned my friendship. You feared to be in my debt." But the man has learned his lesson. The corollary of an eye for an eye is a favor·for a favor. "Be my friend," the undertaker says. No doubt he will call him "Godfather" now, as custom dictates.[29] Don Corleone promptly does his part in the deal; a year later the undertaker gets his chance to redeem the favor he owes him when Sonny Corleone, the Don's oldest son, is riddled with bullets on the highway.

Sonny Corleone (James Caan) meets his end as he waits at a tollbooth. Death comes at him from a waiting car. A man of violent impetuosity, Sonny had waged war against the other Mafia families, and now they have retaliated. That violent nature of his was the main reason that Don Corleone despaired of making him his heir; he would have to find someone else to run the family business. The Don, after all, has his ideals, ideals embodied in the legendary dons of Sicily. As Luigi Barzini in his portrait of the Mediterranean describes these old Sicilian dons, they employ force only regretfully, in order to finance themselves and to enforce their law, which is, in their eyes, the only defense against anarchy. "They are good fathers, good husbands, good sons; their word is sacred; they fastidiously refrain from anything to do with spying, prostitution, drugs, or dishonest swindles. They never betray a friend. They are always devoted churchmen, who give large sums to the local parish or to the deserving poor."[30] They live, in other words, a schizoid life. It is this split that Coppola attempts to dramatize in the character of the Godfather (though Barzini questions whether such a character ever existed among the American Mafia); and he succeeds so well that some critics have accused him of romanticizing organized crime. It is true that *The Godfather* does not follow this split in character to the bitter end; it remains for *Godfather II* to show us that end in the character of Michael Corleone, the Don's third son, heir to the family business.

From a dramatic point of view, *The Godfather* is more the story of Michael Corleone (Al Pacino) than of his father. We meet the father after his life has crested; he is shot rather early in the film and, though still alive, is for all practical purposes put out of action. When Sonny is dispatched for his rashness, Michael inherits the kingdom. There is a second son, Fredo (John Cazale), but he is ineffectual: When his father is gunned down on the street, Fredo is too stunned to do anything except weep uncontrollably. Michael, though best suited, is the least inclined to assume the responsibility of a don. He is best suited because he has inherited his father's cool and has learned intuitively "the art of negotiation," as the family lawyer (Robert Duvall) would put it. He is least inclined because he is determined, at first, to make a life of his own. Against his father's wishes he enlists in the Marine Corps at the outbreak of World War II, becomes a Captain and wins medals for exploits written up in *Life* magazine. (In the novel, when Don Corleone reads about him, he says disdainfully: "He performs those miracles for strangers." The observation is pure Sicilian.) After his discharge, without consulting his father, he enters Dartmouth College, and there he meets Kay Adams (Diane Keaton), an "American girl" whom he actually intends to marry.

What changes everything is the attempt on his father's life. When he goes to see his father in the hospital, he discovers that the detectives that were supposed to be guarding him are no longer there. His father has been set up for another attack.

Later, when he accuses Captain McCluskey (Sterling Hayden) of having been bribed, the police chief smashes his jaw. But Michael will not press charges. At that moment he knows what kind of justice he wants. It is not a justice to be had in the American courts. Once Kay had said to him that it was naïve to think that there was no difference between the tactics of his father and those of a senator or a president. "After all," she says, "they don't make decisions to kill men." To which Michael retorts, "Now who's being naïve?"[31] The decision to kill McCluskey has already formed in his mind. And he carries it out in a scene brilliantly contrived to show the future don's ability to act with cold intelligence, deliberate courage, unblinking deceit, and terrible vengeance. After the murder he flees to Sicily as if to the source. When he comes back, he is the new Godfather. What we have seen is the making of a don. That is why the film is more about Michael than his father. His journey is charted for us from the beginning.

All that is monstrous in the Mafia surfaces in Michael. Don Vito, in his last days, becomes a monster who can scare only children. In another memorable scene, he is playing with his grandson in the dappled light of his garden. He cuts a piece of orange peel and puts it in his mouth. The boy cries, then laughs, and chases his grandfather through a tomato patch pretending to "shoot him down" with a flit gun. Down the monster goes, there among the tomato plants, finally "done in" by a heart attack.

Don Vito's orange-peel trick is part of a pattern that Coppola establishes very early in the film. In every scene depicting or foreshadowing treason or treachery, oranges (or the color orange) figure in some way.[32] In the beginning of the film, for instance, Tessio (Abe Vigoda) is seen at the wedding reception tossing an orange in the air; at the end of the film it is Tessio who betrays the new don, and for his treason is assisted to a waiting car. The key scene, "and the logical motivation for the choice of orange,"[33] is the attempt on Don Vito's life. He is gunned down just after buying a bag of fruit, including the orange which happened to be the first piece of fruit selected. As he falls, oranges spill out on the street from an overturned bucket. Like the pattern of light and darkness, the orange pattern gives evidence of the director's structural control. Sound, as well as image, contributes to this control: Nino Rota's very evocative score, for instance, is skillfully used to mark the varying moods. Because the overall structure is so firmly in place, Coppola can fill his film with a wealth of detail and still not clutter it.

The portrait of the Godfather, as it comes into focus in Michael Corleone, is a miniature of the portrait that Machiavelli drew of the ideal ruler in *The Prince*. The end justifies the means. The end is power, and through power, unity. To achieve this end, everything is permissible, even murder. At the same time, to see and hear him, he is all mercy, humanity, and religion. This duplicity is made quite clear to the viewer toward the end of the film by the intercutting of the baptismal ceremony with the ritualistic murders, in a sequence already referred to. Michael Corleone, answering for his nephew in the role of godfather, renounces Satan and all his pomps even as his henchmen carry out his orders to kill off all his enemies, whose removal is seen as a necessary means to the securing of power. Later, he orders a waiting car for his nephew's father (Gianni Russo) because of that man's complicity in Sonny Corleone's murder. When his sister, Connie (Talia Shire), accuses him of the murder, he insists his hands are clean. When his wife Kay requires further assurance, he faces her squarely and denies all guilt in the matter. But once outside the room, she looks back. Michael's henchmen surround him, kiss his hand, address him as Don Corleone. Kay suspects now what we know. And what we know is that even as he creates around himself his own subservient world he moves toward the hell of his isolated self. This is the course that *Godfather II* will decisively chart.

SLAUGHTERHOUSE-FIVE (1972)

Direction: George Roy Hill
Screenplay: Stephen Geller (from the novel by Kurt Vonnegut, Jr.)
Photography: Miroslav Ondricek

The space-age Everyman of *Slaughterhouse-Five* is Billy Pilgrim, a name that suggests absurdist commentary on Bunyan's *Pilgrim's Progress*. Billy is less a pilgrim than a pawn. His journey, if we can accept the wisdom of the film's space travelers from Tralfamadore, is certainly without progress. Every moment of time is eternally structured. Humans are like "bugs in amber," they claim. Near the film's end, when Russian soldiers liberate Dresden, they find Billy lying helplessly under a huge clock. By then the symbolism is patent: Billy is trapped by time.

As a result of the trauma of being captured behind German lines toward the end of the Second World War, Billy has come "unstuck in time." A prisoner of German soldiers who are all so young they seem like androgynes, Billy is taken to Dresden where he experiences the war's greatest single atrocity. (Kurt Vonnegut patterned Billy's trial out of the substance of his own personal nightmare; he too was a prisoner of war in Dresden at the time of the infamous fire-bombing.) From capture to processing at collection point, from box-car shipment to slaughterhouse-become-concentration camp, from fire-bombing to the excavation of the "corpse mines," the film savors the details of twentieth-century cataclysm. George Roy Hill's humane direction and Miroslav Ondricek's exquisite color photography provide a consistent ironic counterpoint to the script's revelation of man's inhumanity. Of the two utterly senseless deaths it records, one (Edgar Derby's) is the logical conclusion of war's insanity; the other, sadly enough, transcends the divisions of war: Billy's assassin is a fellow American.

The film excels precisely in the technique that typifies the novel's disjointed narrative form. The portrayal of coming "unstuck in time" is at best clumsy in Vonnegut's telegrammatic prose rendering. He resorts to bald statements of transition such as "Billy blinked in 1965, traveled in time to 1958" or "From there he traveled in time to 1965."[34] The initial description of Billy's zany perception of reality reads: "Billy has gone to sleep a senile widower and awakened on his wedding day. He has walked through a door in 1955 and come out another one in 1941. He has gone back through that door to find himself in 1963. He has seen his birth and death many times, he says, and pays random visits to all the events in between."[35]

The film, however, achieves the transitions brilliantly and smoothly through visual association, sound overlap, and the look of outer regard. Its narrative discontinuity begins in 1967, sometime after Billy has been kidnapped and taken by flying saucer through a time warp to Tralfamadore. Billy (Michael Sacks) is typing a letter to the Ilium *News Leader*, describing his life in space. He looks up from the typewriter out the window of his home at the snow-covered lawn and woods: cut to the snowy scene itself, which we quickly perceive is behind German lines years earlier. Billy and three other frozen American soldiers, separated from their company, are about to be captured by the Germans.

The film is so structured that Billy's ordeal as war prisoner from capture to fire-bombing is presented as a straightline though interrupted pattern; it is the film's temporal foundation, and as such it builds quietly but inexorably to the moment of apocalypse. A brief chronology of the major events in Billy's adult life helps to place the film's only continuous sequence (December 1944 through February 1945) in relation to the interspersed scenes that are "unstuck" in the film's visual progression:

> 1944:   (December) Billy comes "unstuck in time" when he and three scouts (Roland Weary among them) are captured behind German lines.
>
> 1945:   (February 13) Billy survives the fire-bombing of Dresden in *Schlachthof-fünf* (Slaught-

erhouse-Five). The middle-aged school teacher, Edgar Derby (Eugene Roche), is shot by a German firing squad for cherishing an undamaged porcelain figurine he discovers in the holocaust's debris.

1948: Billy commits himself voluntarily to the ward for nonviolent mental patients at the Veterans' Hospital near Lake Placid, New York (Eliot Rosewater, the Kilgore Trout fan, occupies the next bed).

1949: Billy marries Valencia Merble (Sharon Gans) six months after leaving the hospital.

1967: On his daughter's wedding night, Billy, at age forty-four, is kidnapped by visitors from outer space and taken to the planet Tralfamadore; Montana Wildhack (Valerie Perrine), earthling movie star, is his zoo mate. Billy's son grows up from hood to Green Beret!

1968: On the way to an optometry convention in Montreal, the chartered plane crashes into Sugarbush Mountain; Billy is the only survivor; he shares a hospital room with B.C. Rumfoord, official historian of the U.S. Air Force. Valencia dies of carbon monoxide poisoning in her Cadillac following an accident on the way to the hospital to visit Billy.

1976: (February 13) Paul Lazzaro (Ron Leibman), fulfilling his absurd promise to avenge Roland Weary's death, kills Billy with a beam from a laser gun while Billy is giving a talk about Tralfamadore in Philadelphia.[36]

The fire-bombing of Dresden is as fine a symbol of apocalypse as recent history has provided simply because of the enormity of its carnage. Dresden was an "open city"; it was undefended because it possessed no significant war industries or troop concentrations. Its art treasures and the splendor of its architecture had gained it the deserved title of "the Florence of the Elbe." To Billy "it looked like a Sunday school picture of Heaven." (Vonnegut admits that it seemed like Oz to him since "the only other city [he'd] ever seen was Indianapolis, Indiana.")[37] What defies explanation is how this massive bombing was hidden from public attention for so long. Dresden was destroyed entirely by what were then considered conventional weapons. Perhaps it escaped notice because it was so shortly followed by the unconventional use of atomic power against two Japanese cities. Yet it remains the greatest single destructive act not only in European history, but also apparently in the recorded history of man-made catastrophes. The atomic bomb dropped on Hiroshima killed some 71,000 people and an incendiary attack on Tokyo (similar to Dresden) caused the death of almost 84,000, whereas 135,000 people died as the result of the attack on Dresden.

The prisoners' entrance into Dresden—a devastating prelude to the horror of its destruction—is one of the film's most stunning compositions of sight and sound. The camera glides past ornamental cornices and Gothic façades; decorative sculptures smile at us and for a fleeting moment we sense the full beauty of man's achievement in the arts. Baroque music accompanies the processional; its intricate modulations complement perfectly the vision of majesty. Even the bedraggled prisoners, their elderly German marshal volunteering in a spirit of former glory, and the troop of youths mustered into the service of a dying cause possess the collective dignity of Isaiah's Israel as suffering servant. The prominence of German children at this stage of our century's second global conflict points ironically to the extremes of man's perversion of society; even youth must be sacrificed for the survival of maniacal greed and dubious freedom. The film *shows* what the novel must *tell*, almost self-consciously: There is nothing so atrocious as expending children for a cause, *any* cause. The novel's subtitle *The Children's Crusade* is occasioned by a captured British officer's comment after he sees the freshly shaved faces of the new American prisoners brought to the camp: "My God, my god . . . It's the Children's Crusade!"[38] The grand result of all eleven Crusades in the Middle Ages (at the cost of two million of Europe's people) was to keep Palestine in Christian possession for about one hundred years! Of these the Children's Crusade was doubtlessly the most ignominious when in 1213 some thirty thousand children volunteered to fight the infidels; half drowned in shipwrecks out of Marseilles, the other half were sold into slavery in North Africa, the planned destination of all.

Planets in science fiction often represent some imagined utopia or heaven. The Tralfamadorians in *Slaughterhouse-Five* (as in two other of Vonnegut's novels, *The Sirens of Titan* and *God Bless You, Mr. Rosewater*) are creatures with special knowledge of the universe (apparently because their technology has permitted them to travel widely enough to know). They claim for instance that "only on earth is there any talk of free will," that only earthlings ask the question *why*. Their stoical determinism accepts the fact that every moment simply *is*; it always has been and always will be the same. There is absolutely no way, they claim, to change the structure of reality. The lesson they offer Billy is this: "Ignore the awful times, and concentrate on the good ones." Tralfamadore and its abduction of Billy and Montana (to observe them mate!) are apparently meant to suggest then that it is possible for man to escape the harshness of reality by living from time to time in his dream world. Montana, star of blue movies, had after all been the object of Billy's occasional sexual fantasies; his only genuine terrestrial solace is his dog, Spot.

Moreover, a significant change in the adaptation from novel to film seems to support this conclusion. The novel ends in the linear temporal sequence with a cautious suggestion of "new birth" after the cataclysm of Dresden. It is springtime, and the war in Europe is over:

> Billy and the rest wandered out onto the shady street. The trees were leafing out. There was nothing going on out there, no traffic of any kind. There was only one vehicle, an abandoned wagon drawn by two horses. The wagon was green and coffin-shaped.
> Birds were talking.
> One bird said to Billy Pilgrim, "*Poo-tee-weet?*"[39]

(This, we had been warned earlier, is all that birds can say in the quiet that follows a massacre.) The film by contrast ends on Tralfamadore, therefore seemingly outside of time, as the camera cranes away from the geodesic dome that houses Billy and Montana and their newborn babe.

Yet somehow it seems hard to accept mere escape from reality as anything other than a superficial interpretation of the

Tralfamadorian sequence; "black humor" at its cynical worst is completely foreign to the film's tone. Concentrating on life's better moments is advice that has more obvious psychological implications. It is closer to a cautious optimism than to a simple denial of reality. Why explore the full horror of total war unless one wants somehow modestly to change the face of things? It is man's pretension that turns technology into the monster that controls him and his fate; one would therefore want at all costs to avoid pretension in proposing a solution to the dilemma of technological man. In the novel it is Kilgore Trout, who in rewriting the New Testament as science fiction, *The Gospel from Outer Space*, suggests an unpretentious program for renewal. The original had never caught on because of a defect in story-telling, Trout claims; it actually taught this: "Before you kill somebody, make absolutely sure he isn't well connected."[40] Jesus, he says, should start off as a nobody and then be adopted as God's son (a theological observation that sounds remarkably like the adoptionist passages in Paul's letters). Then, Trout insists, the proper lesson could be easily taken: "From this moment on, [God] will punish horribly anybody who torments a bum who has no connections!"[41] The film omits this exposition of Trout's work; nevertheless, by its warmly sympathetic treatment of Billy, it seems to capture perfectly the novel's message of tenderness toward abject man. Without proper clothing behind German lines, the prisoners scrounge for whatever they can find. A cloak and silver boots are Billy's lot. He is both Cinderella and Christ; he is Edgar, disguised as a madman, drawing Lear's compassion: "Unaccommodated man is no more but such a poor, bare, forked animal as thou art" (*King Lear* 3:4:110).

In his Preface to *Welcome to the Monkey House*, Kurt Vonnegut, Jr., makes the irreverent claim that his siblings summed up the themes of his novels without actually realizing it. His brother Bernard wrote after his first child was born and brought home: "Here I am cleaning shit off of practically everything." And the dying words of his sister Alice, a terminal cancer patient, were "No pain."[42] The scope of his apocalyptic judgment in *Slaughterhouse-Five*, novel and film, has actually left no significant aspect of our society uncleansed; yet his humor, brilliantly enhanced by George Roy Hill, has indeed achieved that judgment without pain.

Although primarily concerned with war and its senseless and inevitable proliferation of death's horror, *Slaughterhouse-Five* manages in an encyclopedic way to level its sights at an entire world, not unlike ours: against science and affluence, science fiction and middle America, patriotism and marriage, parenthood and free enterprise, fantasy and fascism (individual and collective). Is it inevitable that man's great technological achievements become the inferno of technologism? Are we incapable of controlling our world because we lack the foresight to project the consequences of our scientific dreams? Vonnegut does not, here at least, imagine total catastrophe; he records history. What his humor and the wisdom of Kilgore Trout contribute toward the condemnation of man's pretensions and an expression of hope are more than amply conveyed visually in the warmth of the performances that Hill has drawn from his cast and in the affection with which his camera records even the most bizarre of human tragedies.

NOTES

1. "Arlo's Off-the-record Movie," *Life* 67:9 (August 29, 1969), 8.
2. "Facile Iconoclasm?," *America* 121:5 (August 30, 1969), 126.
3. "Can We Live Together?," *National Catholic Reporter* 6:1 (October 29, 1969), 4.
4. "Leading Back to Renoir," *The New Yorker* 45:29 (September 6, 1969), 96.
5. *Selected Tales and Sketches* (New York: Holt, Rinehart and Winston, 1967), p. 142.
6. Quoted in R. W. B. Lewis, *Trials of the Word* (New Haven, Conn.: Yale University Press, 1965), p. 220.
7. *Newsweek*, October 11, 1971.
8. Ernest Parmentier, ed., *Film Facts* 14:15 (1971), 359.
9. *The New Yorker*, October 9, 1971; for *The Village Voice*, October 11, 1971.
10. Larry McMurtry, *The Last Picture Show* (New York: Dell Publishing Co., 1966), pp. 198-99.
11. *Ibid.*, p. 199.

12. One wonders at times whether the actual places mentioned in the film as within easy driving distance of Anarene—Wichita Falls and Mexico—are not themselves intended to demonstrate the mythic proportions of this Texas town. Archer City, where the location shots were filmed, is of course close enough to Wichita Falls to make Jacy's contacts there appear realistic; Mexico, however, seems well beyond striking distance—for anyone, presumably, other than a Texan.

13. "Some Lessons in Growing Up," in *Film 71/72: An Anthology of the National Society of Film Critics*, ed. David Denby (New York: Simon & Schuster, 1972), p. 90.

14. *Ibid.*

15. Elizabeth Campbell, "Rolling Stone Raps with Peter Fonda," in *Easy Rider*, ed. Nancy Hardin and Marilyn Schlossberg (New York: New American Library, 1969), p. 28.

16. Anonymous, *Films 69/70* (New York: National Catholic Office of Motion Pictures, 1970), p. 19.

17. For an illuminating discussion of the man-machine gestalt, see William Kuhns, *Environmental Man* (New York: Harper & Row, 1969), chap. 6, "The Motorcycle as Persona."

18. *Movies into Film* (New York: Dell Publishing Co., Inc., 1971), p. 116.

19. Tom Burke, "Will *Easy* Do It for Dennis Hopper?" in *Easy Rider*, ed. Hardin and Schlossberg, p. 16.

20. Cf. Eric R. Birdsall and Fred H. Marcus, "Schlesinger's *Midnight Cowboy*: Creating a Classic," in Fred H. Marcus, *Film and Literature: Contrasts in Media* (Scranton, Pa.: Chandler Publishing Co., 1971), pp. 178-89.

21. *Figures of Light: Film Criticism and Comment*, Harper Colophon Books (New York: Harper & Row, 1971), p. 174.

22. "Midnight Cowboy," *Sight and Sound* 38:4 (Autumn 1969), 211.

23. "Ballada O Soldate," in George Sadoul, *Dictionary of Films*, trans., ed. and updated by Peter Morris (Berkeley: University of California Press, 1972), p. 22.

24. *Images of Hope* (New York: Mentor-Omega Books, 1966), p. 30.

25. *Ibid.*, p. 31. While the film has very much to say about man's "hopes," it never directly addresses itself to the question of "fundamental hope." This question is linked inevitably with the young man's death. What does "fundamental hope" mean in a Communist society for the individual hoper? The Golden Age may dawn for a future generation, but what about the individual who must die before it comes? For a response to this question, see Josef Pieper, *Hope and History* (New York: Herder & Herder, 1969), chap. 4.

26. *I Lost It at the Movies* (New York: Bantam Books, 1966), p. 37. But on p. 177, Miss Kael qualifies her dislike of the film: "I didn't much like the material of *Ballad of a Soldier*, but it was well handled to achieve its effects."

27. *The Four Loves* (London: Fontana Books, 1963), pp. 104-05.

28. "Equalizing vengeance" is a term that William F. Lynch, S.J., uses in *Christ and Prometheus* (Notre Dame, Ind.: Notre Dame Press, 1970) to describe the hypothesis operating in Aeschylus's *Oresteia*.

29. There are two words in Italian for "godfather"—*padrino* and *compare*. *Padrino* is the more precise of the two: Its only meaning is sponsor of a child at baptism. *Compare* has that meaning and three others: (1) the groom's best man, (2) companion or friend, and (3) accomplice. The English term "godfather" does not carry the variety of meanings that *compare* does, but when applied to a

man like Corleone it takes on a connotation not to be found in *compare*, namely, his pretensions to godlike powers.

30. *The Italians* (New York: Atheneum Publishers, 1964), p. 268.

31. A number of critics have seen *The Godfather* as a metaphor for American practice in business and government. Perhaps Pauline Kael is more accurate when she says: "In *The Godfather* we see organized crime as an obscene symbolic extension of free enterprise and government policy, an extension of the worst in America—its feudal ruthlessness" (*Deeper Into Movies*, Boston: Little, Brown and Company, 1973), p. 425.

32. For a detailed description of these scenes, see Judith Vogelsang, "Motifs of Image and Sound in *The Godfather*," *Journal of Popular Film* 2:2 (Spring 1973), 118-21.

33. *Ibid.*, p. 118.

34. Kurt Vonnegut, Jr., *Slaughterhouse-Five, or The Children's Crusade* (New York: Delacorte Press, 1969), pp. 45, 43.

35. *Ibid.*, p. 26.

36. The chronology of the film is not noted explicitly; we must and can guess the passage of time from external evidence, historical knowledge, and the effects of time on Billy's face and manner. The date of his death is appropriately an anniversary of the fire-storm over Dresden, the film's and novel's central event. The place is not Chicago as in the novel, but most ironically the City of Brotherly Love. Lazzaro is the ultimate paranoid, in Melville's term for Master-at-arms Claggart a perfect instance of "natural depravity." It is inconceivable that Billy could have been responsible for Roland Weary's death—it was caused by gangrene.

37. *Ibid.*, p. 133.

38. *Ibid.*, p. 97.

39. *Ibid.*, p. 190.

40. *Ibid.*, p. 99.

41. *Ibid.*, p. 100.

42. Kurt Vonnegut, Jr., *Welcome to the Monkey House* (New York: Dell Publishing Co. Inc., 1970), x.

Part Three

THE RELIGIOUS DIMENSION

The religious dimension of man's search for meaning pushes the personal and the social as far as they can go and then comes into its own. If the experience of being loved assures us that we are of value, the love of God not only assures us, but actually creates that value. If we are impelled into communion with others, our relationship to God not only impels us, but becomes the very basis of fellowship.

We experience our relationship to God as Father, Word, and Spirit. The reality of God addresses man as origin and destiny (Father), calls to him to pass beyond himself (Word), and unfolds in the center of his being as a source of creativity and new life (Spirit).

Ultimately, the question of God is not so much, Is there a God, but rather, Is there a God to hope in? Is there a deathless source of power and meaning?

FELLINI SATYRICON (1970)

Direction: Federico Fellini
Screenplay: Federico Fellini and Bernardino Zapponi (loosely based on the work of Petronius Arbiter).
Photography: Giuseppe Rotunno

Although *Fellini Satyricon* is set twenty centuries before the time of *La Dolce Vita* (1961), it presents a vision of deterioration that could only come after its acknowledged sire. Whether its view of a world in utter chaos is to be taken seriously as a statement about contemporary society or simply as the child of a despairing imagination can only be decided perhaps if we can discover a "method" in Federico Fellini's "madness" (or see the film in relation to the enduring health of his imagination in his more recent releases). Fellini himself has indicated that he chose a time before Christ in order to portray the condition of man after the passing of the Christian era. The distance that we feel from the horrors that we see and hear is intended to give us perspective on our own times, obviously not to alienate us from the proceedings altogether.

The film has no plot in the traditional sense of the word; and if its episodes suggest the picaresque genre, the comparison is at best loose because character customarily holds together the segments of a picaresque narrative and Fellini's two youths are purposely kept below the level of personhood. The dualistic pattern of contemporary drama, noted in our discussion of *Scarecrow* and *Easy Rider*, appears again in Fellini's film but with an unusual twist. Encolpio and Ascylto seem at first to be the complementary halves of a single youth. Visually this is true if we borrow our norm from the romance tradition: Encolpio is blond, Ascylto dark. Does one represent spirit, the other flesh; one goodness, the other evil? As the film progresses we discover that they are identical, not complementary halves, and then not even halves. Their ultimate preoccupation is with only a member of the body, its sex.

The episodes are freely adapted from the work identified with Petronius, the "arbiter of taste" in Nero's court, whom Tacitus in the *Annals* calls "a refined voluptuary." Although only fragments of the original have survived the ravages of time, what portions remain (its ending breaks off in midsentence) are clear proof that it was one of the great satirical masterpieces of antiquity. Often considered to be an early example of the novel, Petronius's *Satyricon*, according to William Arrowsmith, "is nonetheless, even in its mutilated state, one of the finest achievements of the Roman imagination, everywhere remarkable for a vigor and vividness and glorious candor that makes it unique in both Greek and Latin literature."[1] The title is probably intended to suggest both "satire" and "satyrs" (i.e., the lecherous or randy). At any rate, it is impossible to decide the exact root of the word and it probably matters little inasmuch as the fragments that we have are both satirical and lecherous.

The way Fellini has altered the shape of the original (as arranged normally by scholars) is undoubtedly significant. What Petronius satirizes brilliantly is the epic form. Just as Odysseus had incurred the wrath of Poseidon (the god of the sea) and was driven over sea and land to learn the ways of man before his homecoming, so the anti-hero of the *Satyricon*, Encolpius ("The Crotch"), offends Priapus (the god of male procreative power) by witnessing his secret rites, is punished with impotence, and is then forced to wander in search of a cure. Encolpius himself makes the comparison to Odysseus; so the basis of this mock-epic parallel is clearly there (Lichas is his Cyclops). The direction of Encolpius's wanderings with his perverse companions is from the vicinity of Naples, by sea and shipwreck, probably to Marseilles—thus, from south to north. Fellini delays the introduction of the epic complication; moreover, he separates the god and the punishment, and changes the route taken by his amorous adventurers to north-to-south. *Fellini Satyricon* begins in the darkness of underground Rome and ends ironically on the sunny sea off the southern tip of the peninsula.

What Fellini preserves and even emphasizes from the extant original, in addition to the principal characters and a few of the memorable escapades (e.g., Trimalchio's feast), is its episodic structure. Although he implies that the fragmentary condition of the original is more the work of Petronius than the rape of time, Fellini insists that our imaginations are stimulated more when we are told less. In an interview he said: "One of the most important aspects of the book for us—to me I think—is just that it is not complete; the author writes in fragments. That is a real stimulus because, if you participate, that book asks your complicity to try to complete all kinds of obscurities that are between one fragment and another one. . . . I try to give the same impression as an ancient fresco in which there are some destroyed figures in one corner. In another corner you see only one hand or one eye."[2]

Indeed, Fellini leaves us with a fragmented fresco as the film's final image. On the shore from which Encolpio and the youths have departed in search of a new world, the blank surfaces of ruined walls are transformed, in the faded hues of Pompeii, into frescoes of the principal characters from the satire. Encolpio's face is only one of many, smiling ambiguously at us from the past, all archetypal credits to the psychic depths of Fellini's imagination. Like the frescoes, the film is, in the words of Stefan Kanfer, "manifestly made for the eye's mind, not the mind's eye."[3]

If Petronius provided Fellini with subject matter for his film, Dante offered the structure. Nor is it surprising that Fellini's palette should be shaded with images and forms from the exceptional literary heritage of his country. Whereas the sense of *Inferno* overwhelms the viewer, its general structure too, though less obvious, can nonetheless be discerned. In place of the figure of Dante, the human spirit in search of salvation, we have, as we noted, bodies in quest of gratification. The plagiarist Eumolpo is a pathetic inversion of Virgil's poetic wisdom as guide. The film begins with Encolpio framed by a wall covered with graffiti; whether ancient Rome or modern subway, the entrance to the underworld shouts the same warning. For Dante it read: "Abandon All Hope Ye Who Enter Here." At the film's end, the cannibalism of Eumolpo's mourners is a sick parody of Satan's meal, itself an appalling perversion of the eternal banquet. And although the sea bearing the youths away

supports a visual allusion to the river Lethe that guides Dante
and Virgil back to the earth's surface, it is highly improbable
that Encolpio possesses the certain knowledge of evil that alone
makes the process of purgation possible.

In Dante's cosmology, hell is a funnel-shaped pit down to
the center of the earth (the crater made by Lucifer when he was
hurled from heaven); Fellini's ancient Italy is a succession of
cavernous mazes: the baths, the Suburra Quarter, the Insula
Felicles (hell as an ancient seven-tiered apartment building), the
hold of Lichas's ship, the underground slave quarters in the villa
of suicides, and the Minotaur's labyrinth. The faces of Fellini's
damned are reduced to lascivious smiles, inviting tongues, and
laughter. The incessant movement of the camera and movement
within the frames—always circular—both draw and repel the
viewer; we cannot remain indifferent to his warning.

Between entrance and exit and beyond images, Fellini has
preserved the structure of Dante's threefold division of hell's
sins—incontinence, violence and fraud. The following outline of
the film's major sequences shows that the principal divisions,
each ending with a fire, can themselves be divided into three episodes apiece.

Exterior wall: Encolpio laments the loss of Gitone.
    The baths: Encolpio and Ascylto fight.

_____(circles of incontinence)_____

Theatre interior: Encolpio wins Gitone back from Ver-
    nacchio.
    Suburra Quarter.
    Collapse of the Insula Felicles: Gitone chooses Ascylto.
Picture Gallery: the poet Eumolpo as guide.
Trimalchio's feast: the furnace for Eumolpo.
    Trimalchio's tomb: the story of the widow of Ephesus.

_____(circles of violence)_____

Lichas's ship: treasures for Caesar.
    The wedding of Lichas and Encolpio.
Assassination of the Emperor: Gitone seized for the new
    Caesar.
Villa of the patrician suicides: the funeral pyre.

————(circles of fraud)————

Nymphomaniac's wagon: a desert area.
Old Temple of Ceres: the death of Hermaphrodite.
  Provincial Arena with labyrinth: Encolpio and the Minotaur.
  Encolpio's impotence with Ariadne, his prize.
Garden of Delights: no cure for Encolpio.

  Oenothea's fire: Encolpio is cured; Ascylto killed in the marshes.
Eumolpo's death: departure for Africa.

The film's introductory sequence shows Encolpio (Martin Potter) searching for Ascylto (Hiram Keller), who has stolen his slave, Gitone (Max Born). Ascylto confesses that he has sold their androgynous lover to the lewd old actor Vernacchio (Fanfulla). The simple acceptance of homosexuality in the film as in Petronius, it should be noted, is certainly neither pornography nor a perverted sexual realism, but a combination of cultural realism, metaphor, and satire.

  The incontinent are the unrestrained; the first three circles reveal the vulgarity of inhumane theatre, the infirmity of art without inspiration, and the excesses of mannerless wealth, each a mask for the diversions of the flesh. Encolpio rescues Gitone from the farting Vernacchio, only to lose the boy once again to his friend Ascylto. Abandoned, Encolpio turns to Eumolpo (Salvo Randone) for companionship and wisdom. The latter laments the death of the arts, yet the museum we see preserves no living past. Complaining one moment about the "greed for money" that has replaced the glorious virtues of "the old days," Eumolpo becomes the next just another sycophant at the banquet of Trimalchio (Mario Romagnoli, "Il More"). Petronius's satire on the social sins of the *nouveaux riches* is perhaps the most widely known segment of his work; Fellini's adaptation of Petronius lays to rest forever the chances for more devastating ridicule.

  The violence of the film's central portion stems from the abuse of civil power: rape, assassination, and suicide. Encolpio is reunited (without explanation) to Ascylto and Gitone in time to be seized by the ruthless Lichas of Taranto (Alain Cuny) and his companion Tryphaena (Capucine), hunter and huntress, combing the seas "looking for precious things to enliven the solitary life of Caesar on his island." Lichas's mock-marriage to Encolpio has scarcely been solemnized when the conspirators, fresh from the assassination of the albino Emperor, behead Lichas himself. Once again without Gitone, taken now as a prize for the new Caesar, Encolpio and Ascylto are consoled for a night by a friendly slave girl in the eerie peace of the villa abandoned by the patrician suicides, loyal to the dead Emperor.

The frauds of the final circles are a dead god, a pederast in Minotaur's clothing, and a garden of feckless delights. An old slave whose mistress is a nymphomanic needing "a man every hour" directs Encolpio and Ascylto to the subterranean temple where the demigod Hermaphrodite "cures people with the plague, can tell you the future better than Apollo." Less potent even than man, the albino hermaphrodite dies in the hands of his greedy abductors. An unlucky visitor to a southern village, Encolpio is forced by the townspeople into the sun-soaked arena of their amphitheatre to fight a Minotaur; the monster after a brief chase succumbs to the charms of Encolpio. Unable to overcome Ariadne (the proconsul has offered her as a prize), the disabled Encolpio is stoned by the people in disgust. Eumolpo, newly rich himself now, appears on a litter and recommends the Garden of Delights, but the therapy of its inmates is insufficient to restore Encolpio's power. Eumolpo is too clearly the remnant of a dying order for his word to save.

The last two sequences of the film—Oenothea's secret and Eumolpo's death—are best understood in the context of Fellini's alteration of Petronius. He delays Encolpio's experience of impotence because he seems anxious to have the film's variations on the sexual metaphor support the process of disintegration that his camera records. Encolpio's journey deteriorates from a quest for a sex object (Gitone), to a flight for survival with his rival (Ascylto), finally to a forced hunt for virility itself. The essential deformity of society, judged piecemeal in successive episodes, is mirrored perfectly in the death of Hermaphrodite, less a statement about the death of God than an acknowledgment of the corruption of human ideals. What hope remains, if any, Fellini anchors in Encolpio's youth and the source of his cure. Oenothea (Donyale Luna), the Earth Mother who restores his sexual powers, is a black woman whose loins preserve life's fire. Not in Petronius's pale north of southern France but only in the sunburnt warmth of Africa come to Italy, Fellini seems to suggest, can we end this apocalypse with hint of renewal. Encolpio's departure for Africa—the Third World—locates the expectation of a new order, in Faulkner's phrase, "in the hot equatorial groin of the world."[4]

Fellini's pre-Christian setting with post-Christian intent effectively reveals what the total absence of values would be like. If man perceives God as his origin and destiny, as Alpha and Omega, precise beginning and definite end, then it is the silence of God we experience in *Fellini Satyricon* inasmuch as it remains forever "in the middle of things," without a clear sense of either beginning or end. It is a movie of visual quest where the *subject* of the search is never really *known*, but only *felt* for awhile as the *object* of sense gratification.

THE PASSION OF ANNA (1969)

Direction: Ingmar Bergman
Screenplay: Ingmar Bergman
Photography: Sven Nykvist

The American title to the film which in Swedish is called *A Passion* is misleading: Anna is not the only one who suffers in the film; if any one character is to be singled out, it should be Andreas. The action of the film begins and ends with him. "This time," the narrator concludes, "his name was Andreas Winkelman." Andreas (Max von Sydow) is Bergman's Everyman. He lives on an island off the Swedish coast,[5] having fled there, it would seem, after his release from prison, where he served sentence for passing bad checks, getting drunk, and resisting arrest. At first his wife, a sculptress, had been with him, but now she has left him, and he is alone with his books.

To be alone is one thing; to be mired in loneliness is another. Andreas does not go under easily. He reaches out to others, but neither he nor they have enough spiritual energy to effect a rescue. He is friendly with Johan Andersson (Erik Hell), a humble woodcutter, but they remain on the periphery of each other's life. He has an affair with two women, Eva (Bibi Andersson), the wife of Elis Vergerus, and Anna Fromm (Liv Ullman), whose husband and child were killed in an auto accident, but with both of them he finds himself in quicksand.

His affair with Eva is brief. She, like him, is caught in her own misery. She thinks she loves her husband, but now she is only "a small part of his general weariness." It is so hard, she says, to realize one day that you are meaningless: "What is this deadly poison that corrodes the best in us?" Later, Andreas will imagine someone saying to him: "You have cancer of the soul." (Outside the door of his house is one of his wife's old statues, a medieval angel made of wood, eaten up from within.) That night he makes love to Eva; the next morning, after she leaves, he lies down on his bed. For a minute there is silence; then he fills the air with the howl of a wounded animal.

If he now lets himself become deeply involved with Anna, it must be with some desperate hope that she, of all people, will know how to heal the wounds of his soul. And yet she, of all people, is most in need. She still limps from an injury sustained in the accident in which her husband and her little boy were killed. The guilt she feels is immense, not only because she had been driving, but because the accident may well have been deliberate. In a dream that explodes in her mind at Easter, she begs forgiveness of a woman who sits by the side of the road, awaiting the execution of her son. The woman angrily pushes her away. Suddenly Anna sees two bodies in a wreck; we see her soundlessly screaming her husband's name.

Her husband, too, was named Andreas, and perhaps it is this coincidence that moves Andreas Winkelman to let down his guard, even after seeing a letter that the first Andreas had addressed to Anna, in which he tells her that in spite of his love for her he must leave her because they cannot help inflicting upon each other "physical and psychical acts of violence." Anna, of course, never alludes to this history of her marriage; in fact she gives out just the opposite, that she lived with her husband in perfect harmony because they believed and trusted in each other. It is this memory alone that sustains her. She cannot imagine how anyone could base a life on cynicism and lies.

Aware of the contradiction, Andreas Winkelman nevertheless takes Anna into his house. Once, before making love, he has his hand at her throat; she says, laughing: "You're strangling me." More and more their love affair becomes a process of strangulation until finally Andreas comes close to killing her with an ax. "When inward life dries up, when feeling decreases and apathy increases, when one cannot affect or even genuinely *touch* another person," says Rollo May, "violence flares up as a daimonic necessity for contact, a mad drive forcing touch in the most direct way possible."[6]

The violence that erupts in the relationship between Andreas Winkelman and Anna Fromm is skillfully reflected in series of violent acts interspersed throughout the film. A killer is loose on the island. A dog is found strung up on a tree; eight sheep are mutilated and left to die in pools of blood. How explain these senseless killings? Who is to blame? One imagines that any one of the islanders is capable of such violence—even the fastidious Elis Vergerus (Erland Josephson), who likes to photograph people in the grip of a wild emotion. Suspicion falls on Johan Andersson, the old woodcutter who keeps to himself and never speaks of his past, and he is bullied into suicide. But a few days after his death, a horse is doused with gasoline and set on fire. The killer is still on the loose. The characters in the film never learn who the killer is, and neither do we. The point has already been made.

Can we give a face to violence? The human face is all we have, and Bergman knows how to play on that. His work in films, he claims, begins with the human face.

> We should realize that the best means of expression the actor has at his command is his *look*. The close-up, if objectively composed, perfectly directed and played, is the most forcible means at the disposal of the film director, while at the same time being the most certain proof of his competence or incompetence. The lack of abundance of close-ups shows in an uncompromising way the nature of the film director and the extent of his interest in people.[7]

Bergman's close-ups of the human face express (sometimes in ways that words cannot) the inner dynamism of his characters. Unlike Fellini in some of his later films, he is not so much interested in a variety of faces as in the variety of things a face can tell. The superiority of revelation through close-ups over more direct attempts is seen at those moments of *A Passion* when Bergman uses the most direct means at his disposal: stopping the film continuity and having the actors step out of their roles to tell us what they think about the character they are playing. Only with deliberate effort and after several viewings can one put together what they have said, and it proves to be nothing more than a confirmation of what the characters have already revealed of themselves in action, with one exception: Bibi Andersson talking about Eva's future. Eva will perhaps become a teacher, she says, a teacher of the deaf, of those who live in deeper isolation than herself, and she will be blessed. At that moment the camera floods her image with light. Earlier, in character, she had said that as a child she had read a book called *Light*. It was all about creation. It made her believe in God.

The use of light throughout the film is masterful, not only for expressing moods but for setting up a contrast between them. The pale light of a winter sun ensnared by fog gives us our first view of Andreas; it soon gives way to the bronze glow of candlelight at a dinner party. When Andreas and Eva first come together, light pours into the room through a red pane in the door, with a warmth of color that seems to radiate from rising flesh; it is followed by the morning's livid light, the sickly hues of regret. The flaming horse in its madness sets a barn on fire, and the screen is filled with a hot luminosity; immediately after, we see Andreas in a speeding car with Anna at the wheel, and the atmosphere is chilled by rain to a gunmetal gray.

Sounds are also given a special value in *A Passion*. Sheep bells are the first sounds we hear, peaceful at first, then melancholy, then somehow ominous. The ticking of a clock is not only the passing of time; it becomes the measure of man's endurance. A charged silence, when Andreas and Anna are on the verge of separation, is made insufferable by the clinking of cups and saucers and the munching of toast. A silence even more insufferable is pierced by a drunk Andreas calling out his name over the winter landscape, as if calling for his lost identity, as if compelled to break a silence in which no God ever calls to him. A foghorn mourns in the distance.

Bergman has written that the individual has become the highest form and the greatest bane of artistic creation.

> The smallest wound or pain of the ego is examined under a microscope as if it were of eternal importance. The artist considers his isolation, his subjectivity, his individualism almost holy. Thus we finally gather in one large pen, where we stand and bleat about our loneliness without listening to each other and without realizing that we are smothering each other to death. The individualists stare into each other's eyes and yet deny the existence of each other. We walk in circles, so limited by our own anxieties that we can no longer distinguish between the true and the false . . .[8]

Even as he deplores this state of affairs, Bergman makes it the object of his concern. It is very much the theme of *A Passion*. And yet, as writer and director, he is not imprisoned by his own concern. Even if his characters remain imprisoned in their loneliness, he suggests that they are made for communion. Even if their wounds are left unhealed, he makes them felt against the wounds of Christ. The title *A Passion* includes the passion of Christ. When the camera moves in on Andreas standing over the body of the persecuted Johan Andersson, it frames him against a picture of Jesus on the wall. When Andreas moves, the camera follows, and each time the picture of Jesus is dimly perceived. Of all the passions that bleed into one another in this film, the passion of Johan, innocent victim, is most like that of Jesus.

But is it redemptive? For himself? For anybody else? In her Easter dream Anna begged for forgiveness but it was angrily refused her. In her last ride with Andreas, after he has attacked her and she has attempted (perhaps) to drive them both to their deaths, Andreas asks her why she bothered to come back for him. She answers: "I came to ask your forgiveness." As he looks at her, he must be thinking either "She is lying" or "If she is telling the truth, I don't have it in me to oblige her." Abruptly, he gets out of the car in the rain and she drives away.

We see him in a long shot pacing back and forth on the muddy road. In one direction is Anna and forgiveness and the torment of achieving communion; in the other direction is his solitary self and exile and alienation. The camera moves in slowly on his pacing. Will we be granted, for a last time, some revelation through a close-up of his face? We never get near enough for that. The image becomes grainier and grainier, and just before it dissolves, we see him fall to his knees in the mud. Over the ticking of the clock comes the narrator's voice: "This time his name was Andreas Winkelman."[9] The ticking of the clock—has it become now the measure of his despair? The despair of ever finding that world of communion in which he could be at home with himself and yet not be alone, and that God who alone could give it ultimacy.

THE SEVENTH SEAL (1956)

Direction: Ingmar Bergman
Screenplay: Ingmar Bergman
Photography: Gunnar Fischer

Ingmar Bergman has more than one affinity to the medieval artist. It is his opinion that "art lost its creative drive the moment it was separated from worship."[10] More than any other film maker, he has concerned himself with religious questions. His concern, he claims, operates on the intellectual level, not the emotional. And yet he knows how to imbue his films with a modern sensibility that engages the heart as well as the mind. The difference between the modern sensibility and the medieval is perhaps the difference between the question and the answer. Bergman knows how to put the question.

The questioner in *The Seventh Seal* is a disillusioned Crusader, a knight of the fourteenth century named Antonius Block (Max von Sydow). Returning to his native Sweden after ten bitter years in the Holy Land, he comes face to face with Death (Bengt Ekerot). In *Wild Strawberries*, Isak Borg meets Death in a dream; Antonius Block meets him as an adversary in a vision. Death appears to him as he does to Everyman in the medieval morality play, but in that play Death is God's messenger; in *The Seventh Seal* Death, when questioned about God, has "nothing to tell." Everyman begs for a reprieve, but is given only time enough to find a companion to go on his journey with him. That companion turns out to be Good Deeds. Antonius Block also asks for a reprieve and gets Death to play a game of chess with him. "I will use my reprieve," he says, "for one meaningful deed."

One meaningful deed. Is that enough to quiet the mind and heart in the face of Death? If only one were sure! If only one could say, No, there is no meaning, Death holds no secrets, there is no God to hope in, there is only emptiness. The knight's squire Jöns (Gunnar Björnstrand) has already reached that conclusion; he has absolutized his need to know. When they witness together the burning of a young girl as a witch, he voices his certainty: "Who watches over that child? Is it the angels, or God, or the Devil, or only the emptiness? Emptiness, my lord!"[11] But the knight cannot bring himself to say so.

"Religious faith," says William Lynch, "has always taught man not only to know, but to be able to live in waiting, in a kind of darkness, making war on the desire of man to reduce the whole of reality, supernatural and natural, to his own limited way of knowing."[12]

For Antonius Block the need to know is all-consuming. In a crucial scene, he kneels by the grill of a confessional, not realizing till the end that Death sits on the other side.

> KNIGHT: Why can't I kill the God within me? Why does he live on in this painful and humiliating way even though I curse him and want to tear him out of my heart? Why, in spite of everything, is he a baffling reality that I can't shake off? Do you hear me?
> DEATH: Yes, I hear you.
> KNIGHT: I want knowledge, not faith, not suppositions, but knowledge. I want God to stretch out his hand toward me, reveal himself and speak to me.
> DEATH: But he remains silent.
> KNIGHT: I call out to him in the dark but no one seems to be there.
> DEATH: Perhaps no one is there.
> KNIGHT: Then life is an outrageous horror. No one can live in the face of death, knowing that all is nothingness.

Death comes up to face him everywhere. Skillfully, Bergman mirrors the central action—the knight's attempt to face Death—in a variety of images, situations, and occasions. Again, as in *Wild Strawberries*, we are continually shifting "from reflector to reflector" throughout the film. When the knight and his squire first arrive upon the scene, they ask a man sitting by the sea to show them the way; he is most "eloquent," as Jöns puts it—he turns out to be a corpse, with empty eye sockets. Juxtaposed to this gruesome reminder of Death's reality is a somewhat comic image: the actor Skat (whose wagon the two travelers pass) putting on a deathmask. But he is so clearly lacking in skill and the mask so crudely made that one almost forgets to fear. Later, thinking to hide himself, the actor climbs a tree, and Death comes to saw him down. A squirrel sits up upon the stump. We smile. Only minutes before we cringed before the death of a young girl, burned at the stake as a witch, and minutes after we are helpless before the death of Raval, a dissolute theologian who ten years before had urged the knight to join the crusade, a victim now of the plague that is ravaging the land. The Dance of Death is ineluctably forming. At the beginning of the film we saw the Dance in a mural in an old stone church; at the end we see it in a vision—Death with hourglass and scythe leading his victims in a "solemn dance toward the dark lands, while the rain washes their faces and cleans the salt of the tears from their cheeks."[13]

The man who so describes this final vision is a simple juggler named Jof (Nils Poppe). He and his wife Mia (Bibi Andersson) make up the entire membership of Skat's "troupe." Of course, says Jof, his son Mikael will grow up to be a great acrobat, or a juggler who will do the one impossible trick. There is no doubt that the three of them are meant to remind us of the Holy Family: Their names Jof and Mia suggest Joseph and Mary, and Mikael, in Hebrew, means "Who is like God." The spirit that lives in this young couple is very different from the knight's. In a quiet interlude, Antonius Block says to Mia: "Faith is a torment, did you know that? It is like loving someone who is out there in the darkness but never appears, no matter how loudly you call." But Mia does not understand him, and Block admits that everything he has said seems meaningless and unreal while he sits there with her and her husband. The faith of this young couple is steeped in love (so unlike the faith of the scornful monk who preaches doom and damnation); and when they open their hearts to him, the knight seems to derive some comfort. Holding in his hands a bowl of wild strawberries in milk, he says:

> I shall remember this moment. The silence, the twilight, the bowls of strawberries and milk, your faces in the evening light. Mikael sleeping, Jof with his lyre.

I'll try to remember what we have talked about. I'll carry this memory between my hands as carefully as if it were a bowl filled to the brim with fresh milk. *(He turns his face away and looks out toward the sea and the colorless gray sky.)* And it will be an adequate sign —it will be enough for me.

Unlike the knight, Jof and Mia never feel the need to stop living in order to ask about the meaning of life. They are the kind Frankl speaks about, for whom it does not really matter what they expect from life, but rather what life expects from them.[14] Jof, for instance, does what he knows best how to do: He juggles, just like that other juggler in the medieval story who performs before Our Lady's altar. And in both instances Our Lady is pleased.

When the knight finally manages to do his "one meaningful deed," it is to do what knights do: He escorts Jof, Mia, and Mikael through the forest and "distracts" Death during the game of chess long enough to get them safely through.

Death wins the game in the end. He comes to the knight as he sits at table with his wife Karin and his squire Jöns and three other companions. Karin is reading from the Bible: "And when the Lamb broke the seventh seal, there was silence in heaven for about the space of half an hour" (Rev. 8:1). The silence, for Antonius Block, is the silence of a God who makes no answer. For the squire Jöns, it means that no one is there. But for the biblical writer, the silence heralds the coming of the Lord.

NAZARIN (1958)

Direction: Luis Buñuel
Screenplay: Julio Alejandro and Luis Buñuel (based on the
             novel by Benito Perez Galdos)
Photography: Gabriel Figueroa

Buñuel, an avowed atheist, has remarked that the perfect
Christian is condemned to defeat. "Christ was crucified after
being condemned. Don't you think that was a defeat?" He is
convinced that if Christ returned, the official voice of the
Church would condemn him. "In a world as badly made as this,
the only path to take is that of rebellion."[15] He may well be
right. But *Nazarin* is not the film to prove it. The portrait of
Nazario, the film's hero, may appear to be that of a true disciple of Jesus of Nazareth in the modern world, but actually he is
the very opposite: Nazario tries to enter into the mystery of love
without loving.

There is no doubt, of course, that Nazario (Francisco
Rabal) is perfectly sincere. He wants to live the life of a priest
in Mexico of the nineteenth century exactly as he imagined
Christ would have lived it. He lives from day to day like the
birds of the air; he gives out of his poverty. He preaches, he
prays, he reproves. But he is immune to heartbreak. There is no
Lazarus to weep over, and his Martha and Mary need not
worry about which one he loves the more; he is equally detached
from them both. One can never imagine him weeping over Mexico as Christ wept over Jerusalem. On his way to Calvary Christ
said to the wailing women: "Don't weep for me. Weep for your-
selves." At the end of the film Nazario receives that grace.

As the film opens, Nazario is living in a crowded tenement.
One gathers that he is held in contempt by most of his neigh-
bors and often taken advantage of. A whore named Andara
(Rita Macedo) is loud in her mockery of him, but when she kills
another woman in a brawl, he takes her in and hides her until
she recovers from her wounds. When she learns that the police
are on her trail, she sets fire to Nazario's room and leaves town

with Beatriz (Marga Lopez), who has just been deserted by her lover. Because of his complicity, Nazario is also forced to flee. Leaving behind his cassock, he sets out on a pilgrimage, with the intention of serving the poor. When he meets up with Andara and Beatriz on the road, he reluctantly allows them to accompany him.

Nazario's journey through the rest of the film is meant to suggest Christ's journey to Jerusalem, where Christ finally meets defeat. Buñuel is masterful in creating for his film an independent reality and at the same time having it resonate with the Christian mystery. That resonance is often ironic, even if Buñuel did not intend it to be so and in spite of what some critics think.[16] The irony consists in this: that Nazario in his dealings with others imagines that he relates to them as Christ would have but in fact does just the opposite. Christianity is, above all, a religion rooted in relationship; Nazario's understanding of it never touches ground.

Consider how Nazario deals with Andara and Beatriz. They play Martha and Mary to his Jesus. There is one scene in which Andara, like Martha (as portrayed in Luke 10:38-41), becomes jealous of Beatriz who, like Mary, sits at the feet of her lord and master and is comforted by his words. Beatriz has just had "a nasty encounter" with Pinto, her former lover (Noe Murayanna), who makes it very clear that he wants her again. "Let me be good, Pinto. Leave me alone!" she begs. But he threatens to come back for her. Now she protests to Nazario that she does not love the man, and yet when he looks at her, she is impelled to do what he wants.

> NAZARIO: It is an evil passion, my child . . . when our mortal flesh cannot be overcome.
> BEATRIZ: And what must one do to kill this evil growth, Father?
> NAZARIO: One must love. Not just one thing, a single human being, but everything that God has made.
> BEATRIZ: Is that how you love, Father? Like you love Andara and me?
> NAZARIO: Yes, like that.[17]

She rests her head on his shoulder and goes to sleep. But Andara has overheard part of their conversation. We hear her sobbing. Nazario calls her over to his side. All the while that he is talking to her, he is looking at a snail that he has picked up from the ground and put on the back of his hand.

> NAZARIO: Tell me what the matter is.
> ANDARA: It's just that everyone has their pride, and one doesn't like to be treated less well than someone else. And you . . . you prefer Beatriz . . . it's not fair.
> NAZARIO: I care for you both equally.
> ANDARA: No you don't . . . You say nice things to Beatriz, but because I am so stupid, whenever you talk to me you just treat me like a fool.
> NAZARIO: Don't talk nonsense, my child. I love each of you as much as the other.

To Martha, Jesus had answered: "Mary has chosen the better part." Jesus no doubt loved all his disciples, but John was the disciple whom, in a special sense, "he loved." If one loves, one is bound to love some more than others. But if one is detached, one is detached from "each . . . as much as the other." The love of God does not dilute our other loves; it transforms them. And when someone comes between us and God, we are told not only to detach ourselves, but "to hate." "If any man come to me and hate not his father and mother and wife and children and brothers and sisters, yes, and his own life also, he cannot be my disciple" (Luke 14:26). To hate, in this sense, is to turn our backs to the one whom we love when that one, wilfully or not, would turn us away from God. Once, when Peter tried to dissuade him from the way he had to go, Jesus said to him: "Get thee behind me, Satan." This kind of hating presupposes a deeply felt love, not only for God but for the one we now must "hate," a kind of love that Nazario had excluded from his life.

Nazario's "charity" is skillfully opposed to the vital human loves of other characters. During a cholera epidemic, Nazario and the two women do all they can to help the sick and the dying. They enter a house in which a young woman named Lucia is dying alone. Nazario tries to get her to confess her sins and to think of heaven. As often as he tries, she answers: "Not heaven. Juan." Juan finally comes; Lucia tells him to send the priest away. To Beatriz, Nazario says: "I have failed." Of course he has, but not in the way he thinks. His failure lies in imagining that love of God is achieved *apart from* and not *through* human love, even a sinful human love (if indeed there is any question of that in this instance). Beatriz says softly, through her tears: "I . . . I once loved like that, too." Maybe so; but her love for Pinto seemed to be more the product of Venus than of Eros.[18] Secretly, however, it is an erotic love that she has begun to feel for the priest; and when she is finally forced to admit it, all her resistance crumbles and she returns to Pinto. We see them together, for the last time, riding off in a carriage, with Beatriz resting her head on Pinto's shoulder in exactly the same way as she had rested it on Nazario's.

Nazario's "charity" is opposed to yet another human love, the love of Ujo the dwarf (Jesus Fernandez) for Andara. There is a remarkable honesty in the relationship between this misshapen little man and the vindictive whore. Ujo will name her for what she is and Andara will mock his deformity; in the other's presence they simply accept themselves and each other. What they feel for each other is affection, the first of the loves that C. S. Lewis describes in his excellent book *The Four Loves*. "Affection," he says, "has a very homely face. So have many of those for whom we feel it." While friends and lovers may feel that they were made for one another, the special glory of affection "is that it can unite those who most emphatically, even comically, are not."[19] Ujo, however, feels more than affection for Andara, though she never reciprocates in kind and never takes seriously his urgent request that she stay with him. In his acts of kindness toward her, he comes closer than Nazario to what is meant by Christian charity because he is clearly more interested in the person for whom he acts than in the action he performs.[20]

Andara is also interested in persons. When she and Nazario are finally taken prisoner, she curses a fellow prisoner who abuses the priest and blesses the one who defends him. To the latter: "May God bless you and give you everything that's good in this world." To the former: "As for you, you filthy coward, may your children rot in their mother's womb and may you choke on pus and die slowly, in frightful pain." She is still in the Old Testament. Nazario, who aspires to the New, finds himself challenged by these same two prisoners, in a way that nothing had led him to expect. They play the bad thief and the good thief to his suffering Jesus. When the former, a parricide, abuses him verbally and physically, the priest says: "For the first time in my life I find it an effort to forgive. I forgive you, because it is my duty as a Christian. I forgive you! But I despise you also, and I feel guilty that I cannot separate scorn from forgiveness." These remarks provoke the parricide to even greater violence. Nazario does not defend himself. At last the "good" prisoner intervenes. Ironically, it is through him that Nazario reaches that point of his crucifixion when he must cry out in his heart: "My God, my God, why have you forsaken me?" Nazario asks him if he would like to change his life. The man surprises him with a question: "Would you like to change yours?" The priest can make no answer. "What use is your life really?" the man asks. "You're on the side of good and I'm on the side of evil. And neither of us is any use for anything."

Nazario is clearly shaken to his very depths. The ground has been taken out from under him. Is it possible that the man is right? Has all his life gone for nothing? Has he actually done more harm than good? Could it be that God never called him? What if there is no God?

In the final sequence, Nazario is taken under special guard to trial. He is in trouble with both Church and State; but as we see him walking along the road, his face reflects nothing but the emptiness within him. A woman is selling fruit by the road, a Veronica set there to comfort him. She offers him a pineapple with her blessing. He looks at her, confused, unable to understand, as if the offer were some obscene intrusion from a world that had already died in his heart. Suddenly a drum roll begins. In the town of Calanda in Spain, where Buñuel was born and raised, the villagers celebrate Good Friday by madly beating on drums until their hands are bloody.[21] Now the drums sound for another *Nazarin* in a Calvary all his own. A second time he refuses. But when she starts away, dejected, he takes her by the arm. We see him in close-up looking at her intently. Then he takes the pineapple and holds it in the crook of his arm like a precious gift. As he goes on his way, his face is wet with tears.

Where is he going, this god at last made man? Wherever, whenever he looks for the one true God again, it will be *through* the human, not apart from it.

THE GIVEN WORD (1962)

Direction: Anselmo Duarte
Screenplay: Anselmo Duarte (based on the play *O Pagador de Promessas* by Dias Gomes)[22]
Photography: Chick Fowle

The Brazilian city of Salvador is popularly known as Bahia, a name it takes from its setting: *Bahia de Todos os Santos*, Bay of All the Saints. The name is appropriate enough. In four centuries the city has raised 228 churches in honor of its saints, while neighboring Recife with a larger population has built only 60. That says something for its religious spirit.

Its religious spirit is a fusion of many spirits. The Portuguese brought with them their own kind of worship, but the African slaves did not leave theirs behind. For every saint whose cult was officially preached, the Africans found a counterpart. They worshiped *Omulu* under the name of St. Lazarus, *Xango* under the name of St. Jerome, *Iansan* under the name of St. Barbara. This identification (or confusion) persists to this day in those voodoo rites known as the *candomblé*.

Against this background the characters of Duarte's *The Given Word* precipitate a conflict that erupts into violence. The peasant Ze (Leonardo Vilar) takes up his cross and walks thirty miles to the cathedral of Bahia only to find that Father Olavo (Dionizio Azevedo) will not let him enter. At that moment the cross becomes, in effect, a battering ram; at the end of the film, weighted with Ze's body, it is actually used against the locked doors of the church. Ze had made a promise to St. Barbara that if Nicholas, his "best friend," recovered from wounds suffered in a storm, he would carry a cross all the way from his farm to the church and place it before her altar. The trouble is he made his promise at a *candomblé* to Iansan, St. Barbara's counterpart. As goddess of lightning and storms, she was the one that had wounded Nicholas; it was to her he had to go.

Nicholas, it turns out, is a donkey. Is he worth all the trou-

127

ble? It is not so much that Ze needs Nicholas for his livelihood. He is poor, but not so poor that he could not afford another donkey. Indeed, part of his promise was to split his land among the destitute farmers, "those without a penny to bless themselves with." No, the reason why Nicholas is worth all the trouble is that he is no ordinary donkey. "He has a man's soul," Ze tells the priest. "He's devoted to me." Whenever anybody wanted to find Ze, they had only to look for Nicholas.

Father Olavo is not moved. To him, it is clearly a matter of principle. The conflict is greater than any two human wills. It is the eternal conflict between faith and superstition, Christianity and paganism, Christ and Lucifer. He brings the matter before the bishop and gets his backing. Ze, for his part, without wanting to, draws to his side the politicians (who exploit him), the reporters (who promote his "cause"), and the common people (who identify with him).

The quality of Ze's resistance is foreshadowed in the opening sequence of the film. We are given close-ups of an assortment of musical instruments as they are vibrantly played in the *candomblé* at which Ze makes his promise. It is a music not easily silenced, and later in the film people dance to it with an aggressive abandon. At one point they stage the *capoeira*, a rhythmic method of fighting with one's feet that is perpetuated in the form of a dance. When the statue of St. Barbara passes in procession, how tame her attendants seem! All of this takes place on the sweeping steps that lead up to the cathedral. Duarte uses them to achieve a kind of visual continuity in much the same way (as one critic remarks) that Eisenstein used the Odessa steps in *Potemkin*.[23] No doubt Duarte also intends their symbolism. As Mircea Eliade notes in his study of religious images, the ideas of death, love, deliverance, and sanctification are all involved in the symbolism of stairs. "The act of climbing or ascending symbolises *the way towards the absolute reality*."[24]

But is Ze's resistance, in the final analysis, anything more than stubbornness, blind pride, sheer presumption? Consider the way he acts toward his wife Rosa (Gloria Menezes). Rosa accompanies Ze on his pilgrimage (compressed into the time it takes to superimpose the credits on the screen) and we see her trudging beside him, obviously irritated by the whole affair. When they arrive at that great sweep of steps that will become Ze's Calvary, Rosa, in utter weariness, mutters: "If all this was for something worthwhile . . . ." Angry and hurt, Ze declares that she did not have to come with him: "When I made my promise, I didn't mention you. Just the cross." But she answers: "I'm your wife. I have to go where you go." Her devotion is soon put to the test. A gigolo named Handsome (Geraldo Del Rey) is determined to have his way with her. Since Ze refuses to abandon his cross, Handsome offers to escort Rosa to a hotel so she can get some sleep. Rosa is aware of the gigolo's intentions, and she is aware of her own readiness to yield, partly out of weakness, partly out of a desire to hurt Ze, and she begs Ze not to let her go. But he senses nothing. One imagines that he is more sensitive to the vibrations of his donkey's soul than to his wife's.

Later, when Rosa returns, she is set upon by one of Handsome's whores, and Ze acts to pull them apart. When the whore impugns Ze's masculinity, he pulls a knife on her. That is as far as it goes, but it is nevertheless a surprising act. Is he actually ready to kill, not to protect Rosa, but to prove his masculinity? Would he kill to get into the church? Is keeping his promise just another expression of *machismo*?

We have to consider the other possibility: that Ze feels he must keep his promise simply because he has made it. God, or St. Barbara, demands it of him. Over and over again, he insists that he has no choice in the matter. Once the promise has been made, he can do nothing but keep it. Even when the bishop sends an emissary to remind him that the Church is authorized to exchange one promise for another, he protests that that would be the same as breaking it. What does it matter if the promise was to Iansan in a *candomblé*? Iansan *is* St. Barbara, and his donkey lives!

Ze, like the priest, is immovable. But one might expect the priest to be more understanding. Ze may be deficient in religious doctrine, but Father Olavo seems to be lacking in religious intuition. Still, he is by no means portrayed as an enemy with nothing good to be said for him. Sometimes we see him as

Ze sees him: in close-up, glowering and frowning. But at other times we see him by himself with rosary in hand, praying for light. Each, in his own way, tries to be faithful.

What does it mean *to be faithful*? To what, or to whom? To oneself? Is fidelity to self the only true fidelity? What is this self to whom one is faithful? When an artist imitates himself, asks Gabriel Marcel, is he being faithful to himself? No, because insofar as he imitates himself, i.e., strives to reproduce, in effect, the same work over and over again, he ceases to be himself. He will continue to be himself only on condition that he breaks free from his work to some extent, only on condition that he responds to a particular inner call which enjoins him not to be hypnotized by what he has already done, but on the contrary to get clear of it and create something new in response to what he hears.

The question for the artist is not very different for man in general. "If I admit without discussion," says Marcel, "that to be faithful to myself means to be faithful to certain principles which I have adopted once and for all, I am in danger of introducing into my life as foreign, and we can even say as destructive, an element as the artist who copies himself does. If I were absolutely sincere I should have to compel myself to examine these principles at frequent intervals, and to ask myself periodically whether they still correspond to what I think and believe."[25] If these principles were to be allowed to stifle my own special reality, how can I be said to be faithful to myself? I would no longer be there, I would not exist anymore, I would have been replaced by a machine. When we look at Ze and Father Olavo, to what extent can we say that each is present to himself, is himself in the other's presence?

Fidelity can never be unconditional, Marcel continues, unless it is a question of faith; he adds, however, that it aspires to unconditionality. For this reason, one ought not bind oneself by oath or promise except in very rare cases. The reluctance to bind oneself by oath is adroitly dramatized by Robert Bolt in his play about Sir Thomas More, *A Man for All Seasons* (later made into a film by Fred Zinnemann). Till the very end More refuses to take the Oath of Supremacy. To his daughter, he says: "When a man takes an oath, Meg, he's holding his own self in his own hands. Like water. And if he opens his fingers *then*—he needn't hope to find himself again."[26]

Ze took an oath, he made a promise. In doing so he gathered his whole self, like water, in his hands. At one point in the film, as the statue of St. Barbara is being carried in procession into the church, she seems to smile at him, and Ze seems to say: "I put myself in your hands." Perhaps, then, his self remains intact, a gift to the God who made men and donkeys, when at the end of the film, caught up in a riot he did not will, he is felled by a shot and his lifeblood is spilt like water upon the cathedral steps. The people lift him upon his cross and carry him into the church, with Rosa following behind.

LA DOLCE VITA (1961)

Direction: Federico Fellini
Screenplay: Federico Fellini, Tullio Pinelli, Ennio Flaiano, and Brunello Bondi
Photography: Otello Martelli

La Dolce Vita like *Fellini Satyricon* is a film with both classical and medieval roots. Whereas the latter finds its classical source, as we have explored in detail, in the secular satire of the Roman Petronius, the former derives its framing images from religious literature, the Book of Revelation. The medieval source for both is Dante's *Inferno*.

The biblical context established by this film's opening sequence immediately provides a firmer basis of hope than Fellini's later apocalypse ever achieves. The statue of Christ the Laborer being carried across the Roman skyline by helicopter is by no means pure symbol; Fellini is too great an artist to do more than suggest the advent of judgment. It is, after all, being taken "to the Pope." This sequence also introduces the film's major images—water and woman—and projects its thematic direction: the nature and cause of the world's judgment. The helicopter carries the statue over the ruins of the San Felice aqueduct, past an apartment terrace where three women sunbathers wave to the statue ("Look, it's Jesus Christ!" one shouts enthusiastically). Then, with the bells of St. Peter's tolling triumphantly, the statue of Christ appears majestically over the great dome of the Basilica (a dome that symbolizes as well as any the *axis mundi* or "center of the earth" for religious man).

Water is of course the first agent of universal destruction mentioned in the Bible. Woman is more evident there as man's companion, yet as his partner too in sin. In Fellini's world, water and woman are everywhere present. Water is a mere reminder of judgment inasmuch as it has lost its complementary capacity to purge, satisfy, and awe (the biblical waters of wrath destroy sinful man while for the righteous they act as the purifying instrument of passage to new life). Woman is the cause of judgment; no longer a companion, she traps man in a web of domination and lust.

If the statue of Christ the Laborer suggests the figure of "someone like a Son of Man" who judges the seven churches, the image of the film's final sequence—the immense, amorphous fish dragged up on the beach, "a strange, bloated monster that stares at us with dead, accusing eyes," as the screenplay describes it—can find its explanation only in the appearance, after the blast of the seventh trumpet, of the appalling beast from the sea (Rev. 13:1) that blasphemes God and his dwelling place; even the ultimate beast of the Apocalypse, "rising out of the earth," whose number is "six hundred and sixty-six," compels all the inhabitants of the earth to worship the other, the beast from the sea. Though we are left with this unequivocal symbol of evil, Fellini would seem finally to emphasize the degradation of man's loss of spiritual purpose rather than the absence of God.[27]

With the film so clearly indebted to the Book of Revelation for its framing images, it was assumed immediately and reasonably—though inaccurately—by a number of critics that there must be seven days of judgment in the film, Revelation's mystical number of completion (there are messages to seven churches, the seven seals, seven trumpets, and seven vials). The contrast of days and nights, which the black-white photography enhances, definitely provides the film's basic structure. However, there are in fact eight nights and nine mornings; and since the succession of day and night is one of nature's cyclic patterns, Fellini seems once again, though more obviously here than in *Fellini Satyricon*, to be indebted to Dante's circles of judgment. The fact that each day judges a different aspect of contemporary society (Rome is simply a metaphor for the modern world) is readily noted; almost invariably too, night offers the opportunity that the following dawn finds sadly inadequate as the goal of man's quest for meaning. Moreover, night's illusory promise is related to a corresponding type of woman. The water that should purge is ever present yet ineffectual. The following outline shows the major events of the series of days and nights (the names of the women are italicized, the uses of water noted):

1 D   Statue of Christ the Laborer carried by helicopter over the San Felice- aqueduct, apartment sun deck, and St. Peter's.

     N   Siamese dancer in an exclusive night club; from Via Veneto to Adriana's flooded apartment with *Maddalena*.

2 D   Marcello's apartment, Emma's overdose; film sex-idol Sylvia Rank arrives at Ciampino Airport, interview at the Excelsior; she climbs the dome of St. Peter's.

     N   Night club in the Baths of Caracalla; *Sylvia* dances with Frankie, the satyr; Marcello pursues Sylvia to the Trevi fountain.

3 D   Dawn at the fountain; fight with Sylvia's boyfriend Robert; Steiner plays a Bach fugue on church organ; the Madonna to appear in a field to two children.

     N   The night of the "media" apparition; no *Madonna* or miracles, only rain, a chaos of cars, and death.

4 D   Last rites for a dead man at dawn.

     N   Party at Steiner's apartment; the sound of the sea on tape; intellectuals court the *Muse*.

5 D   A seaside restaurant at Fregena; Marcello seeks peace to write; the little "Umbrian angel," Paola, serves table.

     N   Marcello's father, in from the country, on the Via Veneto; to his favorite Kit Kat Club (tigress chorus line; the cornet clown, a Pied Piper with balloons) and *Fanny's* apartment.

6 D   Marcello's father's heart seizure.

     N   Aristocrats' party at the castle of Bassano di Sutri; Maddalena proposes through the shell fountain; the American painter *Jane* and other guests hunt ghosts by candlelight in the abandoned villa.

7 D   Prince Mascalchi's mother goes to Mass as debauchers return.

     N   Highway outside Rome, Marcello and *Emma* argue, are reconciled.

8 D   Marcello's apartment, with Emma; the discovery of Steiner's suicide.

N   Orgy at a villa in Fregena; *Nadia's* striptease.
9   D   The sea monster brought up on the shore;
        Paola waves to Marcello.

Marcello (Marcello Mastroianni), a newspaperman, is
Fellini's representative modern man. Although his talent is apparently adequate to a more serious form of writing (Steiner
inquires about the book he is supposed to be writing), he allows
himself to be drawn into the vortex of sensational journalism.
Wherever the ephemeral news story breaks, he is there, accompanied by his photographer friend, Paparazzo (Walter Santes-
so). Where the leads are unreserved, the newsmen are present en
masse; their photographers swarm like flies around the carrion
of titillation. Marcello's pursuit of excitement in the news inevitably becomes a stimulus to sexual conquest.

Thus as Marcello and Paparazzo follow the helicopter carrying the statue to the Vatican, their attention is easily diverted
to the sunbathers on the apartment roof; Marcello's story of the
morning would be incomplete without the personal satisfaction
of getting their phone numbers. The famed (or infamous) Via
Veneto is Marcello's real "beat," the center of Rome's "sweet
life." The first evening, while in an expensive night club observ-
ing the conduct of a vagrant Roman prince, Marcello renews
contact with Maddalena (Anouk Aimee), a nymphomaniac
heiress. They offer a friendly prostitute Adriana (Adriana Mon-
eta) a ride home and furtively (though urgently for Maddalena)
indulge their liaison in her flooded basement apartment. A pre-
carious plank-walk leads to their ludicrous ark, a prostitute's
bed. There is scarce comfort from the flood in the arms of the
wealthy. The momentarily sated Marcello reaches his own
apartment in the early morning hours just in time to save his
mistress, Emma (Yvonne Furneaux), who has taken an overdose of pills.

The superficial pursuit of news the second day lures Marcello into the orbit of film stardom. Sylvia Rank (Anita Ek-
berg), cinema's currently reigning sex goddess, descends upon
the capital of the Christian world ("You like the Eternal City,
Miss Rank?" a reporter asks), rides triumphally from airport to
city, and vigorously ascends the dome of St. Peter's—with ex-

hausted men in her wake—to give her blessing *urbi et orbi* from its balcony. The appointed high priestess of sex is, of course, appropriately dressed in naive clerical fashions, a black cardinal's hat and a white Christian Brother's bib at the modest neck of her long black dress. Just as she becomes aware of the handsome Marcello at her side, a gust of wind sweeps her hat down into the square below. That evening, more suitably attired to reveal her endowment as Earth Mother, Sylvia is once more the center of attention, now in the cavernous ruins of the Baths of Caracalla-become-nightclub. While her fiancé, Robert (Lex Barker), and Marcello watch, she is literally swept off her feet by Frankie Stout (Alan Dijon), a sinuous young dancer, bearded like a satyr. They resemble two young animals preparing to mate. Later, Marcello rescues her from an argument with her drunken fiancé and rides off into the night searching (he thinks) for a trysting place, with the evident pleasure of one who has mounted Olympus itself. He has sadly misunderstood his prize though. Sylvia is more innocent child or harmless animal than sacred prostitute of the movie industry. On a country road, she is fascinated by the howl of a dog and returns his call; they are instantly routed by an awakened pack. Back in the city, she makes Marcello look for milk for the kitten she discovers, begins to caress, but puts aside as her infantile span of attention turns abruptly to the glories of the Trevi fountain. Refreshed by the spray of the fountain, Sylvia stretches out her arms to receive the returning Marcello. No sooner has she sprinkled him with water when the fountain is turned off and silence descends at dawn to mock their meaningless rite of initiation. Back at the Excelsior, Marcello must pay even more for his self-indulgence than the night of frustration as Robert slaps Sylvia and levels him with one punch.

The events of the third day show how the Church itself can become the pawn of sensationalism; its piety has always been subject to superstitious distortion. Two children have reportedly seen the Madonna. Invalids, pilgrims, and the idly curious gather in a field for her expected reappearance. Photographers and TV cameramen erect scaffoldings for their lights to assure perfect preservation of the apparition on celluloid. As rain begins to drench the children and the spectators, and the flood-lights explode, the children create pandemonium when they mischievously dash from the "miracle tree," this way, then that, shouting, "There is the Madonna!" The field becomes a chaos of cars, lights, horns, and the cries of frightened people. The night's only accomplishment is the death of an invalid. In the dreary light of a cloudy dawn, a priest who had rejected the claims of the children chants the prayer for the dead. The one who needs it least lies motionless on a stretcher. Man's presumptuous attempts to force God's hand lead only to tragedy.

Steiner (Alain Cuny), with the apparent composure of one who has fully integrated life and work, entertains his friends at a party on the fourth night. They are all, with the exception of Emma, artists, writers, intellectuals, devotees of the Muses. An Indian girl, playing the guitar and singing, draws a compliment from the robust, sage Rapaci. "The only authentic woman is the Oriental woman," he insists. "Mysterious, maternal, lover and daughter at the same time, the Oriental woman delights you by crouching at your feet like a tiger in love." The Garden of Eden and Eve were, after all, "in the East." Instrument, song, and conversation allude perhaps to the special attendance of Erato with lyre, the Muse of love poetry. (The name itself suggests ironically a judgment of their erratic lives.) The Englishman Desmond, secretly recording their conversation on a tape that Steiner has made of nature's sounds, plays back to the assembled group the unexpectedly poignant juxtaposition of thunder, the voice of the sea, birds, and wind in the trees with Steiner's sad admission (holding thumb and forefinger slightly apart): "If you see me as I see myself, you would know that I am not any taller than that." Despite evident warning to the contrary, Marcello (as well as the viewer) is inclined to feel that here at last is some haven of meaning in the midst of disorder. He calls Steiner's home "a real sanctuary" and asks if he may come more often.

Influenced no doubt by this intellectual interlude (though Steiner had confessed, "It is peace that makes me afraid. . . . I feel that it's only an appearance, that it hides a danger"), Marcello begins the following day at a seaside restaurant in

Fregena, typewriter and paper at hand, insisting, "I want to work in peace." He is attracted by the fresh and innocent beauty of the young Umbrian girl Paola (Valerie Ciangottini), who works in the restaurant. "You remind me of one of those little angels in the churches of Umbria," he comments. Paola, associated with the sea in both her appearances in the film, here and at its conclusion, is Marcello's graced invitation to the genuine peace of spiritual renewal.

That night, the fifth, Marcello meets his father (Annibale Ninchi) on the Via Veneto; he is in Rome for a day, wanting apparently to renew some of his former nocturnal acquaintances as much as, if not more than, to see his son. Their adult companionship is little more than connivance in adolescent infidelities; the father's conscious concern for his son is limited to a passing comment about the infrequency of his letters and visits home. Yet their reunion provides the film's warmest, most touching episode. At the Kit Kat Club, the old night club of his father's choice, the delights are serene and definitely dated; sex is there in a lower, though hardly baser, key. A clown cracks a whip at a line of chorus girls in scanty costumes and tigress masks. The "Twenties" atmosphere continues as the girls return in flapper dresses and cloche hats, holding big balloons that abandoned become in the final act children obedient to the sad summons of the clown's Pied Piper's horn. Though it is the father's preference for clubs, Marcello knows one of the girls. Fanny (Magali Noel) later invites his father to her apartment for more, we can safely assume, than the announced spaghetti Bolognese. Called back suddenly in the early morning hours, Marcello finds his father depleted and much older, yet insisting that he return home at the appointed hour. His heart attack is by no means merely a physical failure.

The sixth circle reveals the degeneracy of Roman aristocracy; the guardians of tradition are pasty ghosts haunting the villas of the past. The activity moves once again from the Via Veneto, this time to a party at the castle of the fiancé of another of Marcello's friends. Massive busts of ancient Roman senators and emperors line the high-ceilinged hall at Bassano di Sutri; the cadaverous aristocrats who move dreamily through the room are scarcely more alive. Maddalena offers Marcello a tour through a gallery, down a cavernous corridor, into a room she calls "the chamber of serious discourse." Leaving him there, she returns to a shell fountain in the hallway beneath the statue of a nude woman. It is not just a fountain, but also a mouthpiece that carries even her whisper back to Marcello's room. While she proposes marriage and Marcello seems receptive, a young man approaches her; separated from Marcello, still isolated in the echo chamber, they begin to make love. Opening the nearest door, Marcello is swept along with the group joining the American painter Jane as she leads a silly candlelit search for actual ghosts. The emptiness of Marcello's "discourse" with Maddalena is doubly clear when he uses the willing Jane for his dark purposes in an abandoned villa. As the revelers return at daybreak, the prince submissively and hypocritically joins his mother in another procession—into the chapel for Mass.

As passionate as the conflict of the seventh night is, its cast is deceptively simple: Marcello and Emma argue in a parked car on a highway outside Rome. In more ways than one it is the calm before the final storm. Emma insists that he has found without realizing it "the one thing necessary"—a woman who loves him as if he were the only man in the world. Her love, he responds, is "aggressive, sticky, maternal"; he accuses her of knowing nothing but "the kitchen and the bedroom" as if he were not even more severely limited, in action at least, by his obsession with the latter. He abandons her to the night, wanting never to see her again; when he returns in the daylight to retrieve her, one wonders if it is not simply for the gratification of frustrated animal need. Their brief rest is broken though by the call announcing Steiner's suicide.

The staircase that Marcello climbs to Steiner's apartment, lined with newsmen and curious onlookers, spirals up; the camera's angle catches nine levels, another modern instance of Dante's pit. Leaving no further explanation than the tape of his voice and the sounds of nature, Steiner has taken the lives of his two children and his own. The photographers converge on his wife like vultures as she returns to the apartment, unaware of the inexplicable tragedy that has annihilated her family.

The seaside orgy of the eighth night shows the utter depravity of "the sweet life." Night, boredom, and sex have brought together a motley assortment of degenerates. The ostensible reason for the gathering is to help Nadia (Nadia Gray) celebrate her annulment. Marcello proposes the fitting toast: "To Nadia. . . . To the annulment of her marriage, to the annulment of her husband, to the annulment of everything." As if to annul herself, Nadia agrees to entertain her guests with a striptease. Although Marcello comments sardonically that the dance will "baptize her in her new life," the performance, however inept, is by no means the nadir of the evening. (Even the music is debased; the song "Patricia" was earlier associated with Marcello's Umbrian angel.) Transvestite homosexuals, in sequined ballet dresses, do a chorus routine to the tune of "Jingle Bells." When Marcello, hopelessly drunk, presumes to entertain the guests, he cruelly sits astride Pasutt, a fleshy blonde, and rides her like a horse, using her slip strings as reins. She collapses; he tries to slap her back to consciousness. As the wild tempo of the party begins to dissipate (the lights dim and the film's haunting theme returns), the last semblance of human dignity and personal respect is drained from the scene. Marcello, whose animal urges women have yielded to in kind, shows at last the full degradation implicit in his life: He sadistically insists on making a chicken of Pasutt, pouring water on her inert body, then pasting feathers from a ruptured pillow on her face and throat.

One by one, as if on cue, the couples make their exit from the villa into the dawn of the ninth and final day. The timing of their last judgment is precise. As they reach the beach, the "beast from the sea" is being dragged up on the shore by fishermen. In the depth of the pit is the manifest image of their bestial depravity. The hideous reality of their lives that we have come to know in deepening circles they are now allowed to glimpse. While the round, dead eye of the fish stares back, they gawk—incredulously. Across an inlet, children are playing. Paola, the Umbrian angel, waves to Marcello and calls, but the wind and the sea carry her voice away. Marcello's response is the pathetic self-indictment of a hardened heart, of an ear deaf to the call of grace: "I don't understand. I can't hear." Paola smiles and waves; she continues to smile as he walks away. It is this symbol of hope Fellini leaves us with.

On nine successive days, the Eternal City becomes Dante's City of Dis, displaying its damned in vicious circles of frustrated opportunity. The modern world offers man the possibility of wealth, stardom, religion, art, family, tradition, love, debauchery, and finally grace as sources of personal meaning. Each offer is rejected: the first eight because, debased by "the sweet life," they are empty illusions, void of meaning; the last because man himself is empty. The fire of his spirit has been extinguished by his insatiable animal desire for woman, who is either present and all-consuming or simply silent.[28] Nature mirroring society has lost its capacity to rejuvenate man's spent energy.

The Spirit of God presents himself to man as a summons to creativity and new life. If modern man does not answer the call to transcend his baser urges, it is not, Fellini insists, because the invitation is no longer made. Man's sensitivity to the voice of mystery has been deadened by the clamor of his flesh. His quest for meaning is nothing more than aimless drifting.

2001: A SPACE ODYSSEY (1968)

Direction: Stanley Kubrick
Screenplay: Stanley Kubrick and Arthur C. Clarke
Photography: Geoffrey Unsworth, B.S.C.

"What shall this child be?" This question, asked of John, the baptizer-to-be, is asked of every child. With special wonderment it is asked of the Star Child at the end of Kubrick's space odyssey, a fetus enclosed in a transparent sphere as great (in the eyes of the camera) as the earth and given (in the final shot) a seeming ascendancy over it. Where does he come from? What is he? Where is he going?

2001 is preeminently a visual experience. Out of two hours and nineteen minutes of film, there are only about forty minutes of dialog. As Kubrick declared, he intended the film to be "an intensely subjective experience that reaches the viewer at an inner level of consciousness, just as music does."[29] It is music, in fact, that dominates the opening of the film: The great chords of Richard Strauss's *Thus Spake Zarathustra*, an aural symbol for all that follows, seem to generate an upward thrust even as they establish themselves horizontally.[30] As we hear this music, we observe what Kubrick calls the "magical alignment" of heavenly bodies: From the viewpoint of the moon we see the crescent of the earth appear and then the sun in a burst of glory. A similar configuration will herald every call (but one) to the human spirit. Here, it heralds the birth of that spirit.

"The Dawn of Man" is the first of four episodes, three of them titled. A second episode (whose title is clearly sacrificed to the power of an image) is closely linked with the third: "Jupiter Mission: 18 months later." The last episode is titled "Jupiter and Beyond the Infinite." There occurs in each episode a crucial interface. Interface has been defined as the process initiated by the contact between two systems. "In all cases," says William Kuhns, "the interface is capable of catalyzing a new synergetic level of relationship between the two systems—one, that is, con-

taining more than could be predicted through a separate knowledge of the two systems."[31] In the first episode the interface is
between mind and matter; in the second and third it is between
man and technology; in the fourth it is between man and God
(or the Infinite).

The first episode, "The Dawn of Man," is in its own way a
retelling of the Book of Genesis. In the beginning the earth is a
desert of silence. Light is separated from darkness and the
waters have crawled back into their holes where beasts gather to
eat and be eaten. A tribe of apes moves ineptly among them.
One of them, who can scream louder than the rest, is clearly
their leader. Still another trait singles him out: He is strangely
fascinated by the moon, and so the script calls him Moon-
Watcher (Daniel Richter). Something is abroad in the land,
some alien spirit filling the night with its presence. One morning, suddenly, mysteriously, a great black rectangular monolith
(lit from behind and photographed from below) towers in the
midst of the apes. Moon-Watcher's eyes are riveted, but now he
looks out through them as if from some inner eye. When he
moves forward, with something akin to fear and trembling, in
order to touch the apparition, the journey of the human spirit
has begun.

The appearance of the monolith is made to coincide with
the rising of the sun and the waning of the moon, all three in
that prophetic alignment seen in the opening of the film. It is
accompanied (as it will be in all subsequent appearances) by the
music of György Ligeti's *Requiem*, as if to suggest the partial
deaths and resurrections man must undergo in his climb to the
stars. The monolith itself hums with an energy so compelling
that nothing, it seems, can touch it and not be changed. What is
this apparition? In Arthur Clarke's novel, which Kubrick insist-
ed should not be published until after the release of the film, the
monolith exists mainly on the narrative level; in the film it
vibrates with a greater resonance on the level of meaning. In the
novel it is, for all its complexity, quite simply a machine, one of
several planted by alien intelligences all over the earth, compu-
terized to effect the evolution of the apes. Kubrick very wisely
excised from the film almost every bit of narration that would

lock the monolith into this explanation. He does not exclude such an explanation, but he lets the monolith stand in its own mystery, a mystery that is never absent from the interface between mind and matter that it initiates. In the film it functions symbolically, perhaps as "that energy which, having generally agitated the cosmic mass, emerges from it to form the Noosphere,"[32] to use the words of Pierre Teilhard de Chardin. Certainly it suggests the infinite, the inexhaustible, or what we call God, the power of the future.[33]

What does Moon-Watcher do with that burst of sunlight behind his eyes? He begins making connections—a bone becomes an extension of his hands, becomes a tool, becomes a weapon, becomes the instrument of his survival. Consciousness gives birth to both good and evil. Moon-Watcher becomes both Cain and Abel. Cain goes unpunished, as Clarke notes; but from that moment on, all the good that descends from violence is inextricably tied to the evil that violence produces. Insofar as man profits from the good, is he not guilty of the evil?[34]

Another question surfaces with the first burst of intelligence. What is its relation to feeling? Technology, however primitive, is born of intelligence abstracted from feeling. What if that separation becomes a divorce?

Both questions—of good and evil, of feeling and intelligence—leap four million years into the next (untitled) episode of the film, which begins with a masterful match cut: Moon-Watcher flings his weapon high into the air and the falling bone turns into an orbiting satellite. First the earth becomes visible; then a wheeling space station, toward which a space ship is moving. This time it is Johann Strauss who provides the music: Kubrick found his "Blue Danube" ideal for depicting grace and beauty in turning. At the same time, we are given, as Carolyn Geduld notes, a classic example of what Eisenstein and Pudovkin call an orchestral counterpoint of visual and aural images. "Instead of merely paralleling the effect of drifting space vehicles with music appropriate to outer space, the waltz, because it is both appropriate and inappropriate, serves as a commentary on the nature of space travel in the twenty-first century: measured, polished, choreographed, routine."[35]

On the spaceship *Orion* we see "what evolution hath wrought": Dr. Heywood Floyd (William Sylvester) is a fine specimen of twenty-first century man. As Moon-Traveller, he is very different from Moon-Watcher, and yet also the same: He is surely endowed with feeling and intelligence, but we sense that in the cold world of space the separation between these two expressions of man's being has been systematically institutionalized. Men seem isolated from one another, impersonal in their relationships. Detached and pleasant, Dr. Floyd travels to the American moon-base located in the crater Clavius. The purpose of his mission is to investigate the discovery of a top secret object, a "rock" of some kind, recently excavated, that seems to have been deliberately buried some four million years ago on the moon. When he and his colleagues gather around it like priests around an altar, we know what they do not: The "rock" is identical to the monolith that descended upon the world of the apes. Moon-Traveller does what Moon-Watcher did: He touches it, just as the sun rises over it, and at that moment it emits a powerful hum that sends him reeling.

The hum is a radio signal that is tracked to Jupiter, and so begins the mind-bending space odyssey of the title. In Episode Three ("Jupiter Mission: 18 months later") the spaceship *Discovery*, resembling in form the vertebrae of some future specimen scooped out of the stars and yet related to that first bone shot into the air, moves through the great calm of space to the adagio of Khatchaturian's *Gayane* ballet suite. It carries a crew of six: Mission Commander Dave Bowman (Keir Dullea) and his assistant Frank Poole (Gary Lockwood), three hibernating scientists, and a computer named HAL (Douglas Rain as HAL's voice). In the deadly routine of space travel, feeling is of necessity suppressed, but even intelligence seems to be marking time. Intelligence has been entrusted to the computer HAL, and ironically it is HAL who lets his feelings get in the way. "Among the masterstrokes of the episode," says Geduld, "are Kubrick's well-placed 'subjective' shots *through* the computer's eye and also *of* the computer's eye, indicating exactly what HAL is thinking."[36] And feeling.

Apparently for reasons of security, HAL is the only one of

the three functional crew members who knows what *Discovery's* mission is all about: the tracking of that radio signal to Jupiter. The computer is programmed to serve man; but in giving it knowledge man, it seems, has unwittingly programmed in his own desire to control. In the depths of space, therefore, HAL attempts to take over. Through a series of artful maneuvers he gets Poole out on a space-walk and severs his air hose; he deliberately shuts off the lifeline to the three hibernating scientists; he tries to prevent Bowman's reentry into the spaceship when the latter returns from an unsuccessful attempt to rescue Poole.

Visually, as Geduld points out, the sequence is a culmination of the abstract uterine imagery used throughout the film. At this point heavy breathing replaces the musical score on the sound track, communicating on one level the turmoil in Bowman's psyche (does it take the threat of violence now to awaken man's feelings?) but suggesting on another level the effort of beginning life. *Discovery* is seen as the *mother* ship that gives birth to the infant pod and later to Bowman himself as he emerges head first with the two great eyes of his helmet staring out at us through space. "The whole sequence represents an abstract childbirth in space anticipating the birth of the Star Child."[37]

Bowman bypasses the skills of his recalcitrant computer and blasts himself back into safety. He knows now what he must do. He systematically disconnects the vast network of HAL's memory center, undeterred by HAL's carefully modulated protests and by the whining of his winding down. Immediately after (by coincidence?) a prerecorded briefing flashes on a screen, and Dave Bowman learns for the first time the true purpose of the mission.

Ligeti's music carries us into the fourth and final episode of the film: "Jupiter and Beyond the Infinite." Going before us like a pillar of fire is a third monolith, lit by Jupiter's sunrise. Bowman follows after it and then plunges into the kaleidoscope of what we imagine to be Jupiter's atmosphere (effected by a special slit-scan machine designed by Douglas Trumball) but which Clarke, in his novel, describes as the inside of the monolith. Perhaps Kubrick means to suggest this by the rectangularity of the light. At any rate, Clarke, in his novel, has Bowman approach the monolith spotted on one of Jupiter's moons and enter what he calls the Star Gate. "Impossibly, incredibly, it was no longer a monolith rearing high above a flat plain. What had seemed to be its roof had dropped away to infinite depths; for one dizzy moment, he seemed to be looking down into a vertical shaft," and Bowman cries out (not in the film, but in the novel): "The thing's hollow—it goes on forever—and —oh my God!—*it's full of stars!*"[38]

So where does he end up, after this hair-raising trip? In an elegant green-and-white suite of rooms (which some critics identify as Louis XVI or eighteenth-century but which Clarke simply describes as an "anonymous hotel suite that might have been in any large city on earth"). In these strange/familiar surroundings Dave Bowman, in solitude, undergoes a series of transformations, involving him in a process of aging that brings him to the brink of death. At that point a fourth monolith appears, enveloping him in cloud. The transformation that takes place now is the most startling of all. As the great chords of *Zarathustra* begin their ascent once more, the Star Child is born, rising in global splendor above the earth.

"What shall this child be?" The answer to the question is perhaps as enigmatic and as full of the future as God's answer to Moses from the burning bush: "I will be what I will be." This child is *called* to be. A reality greater than his own addresses him as origin and destiny, commands him to pass beyond himself, unfolds in the center of his being as a source of creativity and new life.

NOTES

1. "Introduction" to Petronius, *The Satyricon*, trans. by William Arrowsmith (New York: New American Library, 1959), v.

2. *Federico Fellini*, Discussion No. 1, A Publication of the Center for Advanced Film Studies (The American Film Institute, Inc., 1970), p. 7.

3. "Rome, B.C., A.D.," *Time* (March 16, 1970), 76.

4. *Absalom, Absalom!* (New York: Modern Library, 1936), p. 116.

5. The island where Bergman lives has served as the location for three

other films: *Shame, Hour of the Wolf*, and *Persona*.

6. *Love and Will* (New York: W. W. Norton & Co., 1969), pp. 30-31.

7. Ingmar Bergman, *Each Film Is My Last* (New York: Janus Films, undated), p. 6.

8. "Introduction," *Four Screenplays of Ingmar Bergman*, trans. by Lars Malmstrom and David Kushner (New York: Simon & Schuster, 1960), xxii.

9. "This time" can be taken to mean "in this film": In that case Andreas Winkelman (as we indicated earlier) is seen as another embodiment of Bergman's Everyman. But "this time" should also have a meaning purely in the context of *A Passion*: "This time the Andreas that Anna almost killed was Andreas Winkelman," suggesting that the second relationship was a kind of replay of the first. Vernon Young, in his provocative study of Bergman and the Swedish ethos, *Cinema Borealis*, goes further: He thinks Andreas Winkelman and the other Andreas are one and the same. "The place to recognize this fact is precisely where it is given: at the beginning when Anna uses the telephone, calls Elis, and refers to 'Andreas.' If you let this go by as if it were a coincidence, then simply decide later that you are seeing a kind of fatal retake of a previous relationship between Anna and the other Andreas, you will never get untangled. What Bergman has done in this film is to abdicate from the conventional conception of time and duration, even more radically than he did in *Persona*. This is *limbo* or, if you like, purgatory. This has all *happened before. It will happen again. Time is spiral.* Andreas and Anna and the others are *reenacting* a convoluted, unending torment, out of the time-space continuum we are prepared to accept" (New York: Avon Books, 1971, p. 267). Young makes this claim in spite of such discrepancies as a photograph of the first Andreas that does not resemble the second at all. He sees this as an attempt by Bergman to deceive us or as an indication of his indifference to visual logic.

10. "Introduction," *Four Screenplays of Ingmar Bergman*, xxii.

11. All quotations of *The Seventh Seal* are taken from *Four Screenplays of Ingmar Bergman*.

12. *Images of Hope* (New York: Mentor-Omega Books, 1966), p. 98.

13. There is some discrepancy here between image and word. We see seven figures in the dance of death. Death is surely the first figure, and Skat is the last. Who are the other five? Death, we are led to believe, takes all who are in the castle with the knight—his wife, his squire, a blacksmith and his wife, and a simple girl. But one of the women is missing from the five. And Jof, in his vision, says that he sees the knight and his squire, the smith and his wife, and Raval and Skat.

14. *Man's Search for Meaning*, p. 122.

15. Quoted by Raymond Durgnat in *Luis Buñuel* (Berkeley: University of California, 1967), p. 112.

16. *Ibid.*, p. 109. Says Durgnat: "It seems that a film has only to repudiate orthodox Christianity to be felt to be ironic, simply because so many spectators impulsively grant Christianity a sentimental respect. When the film ceases to indulge it, they feel that they have somehow been tricked by an ironist."

17. All quotations of *Nazarin* are taken from *The Exterminating Angel, Nazarin, Los Olvidados*, three films by Luis Buñuel, trans. by Nicholas Fry (New York: Simon & Schuster, 1972).

18. The reference here is to a distinction made by C. S. Lewis in his book *The Four Loves* (London: Fontana Books, 1963). "That sexual experience can occur without Eros, without being 'in love' and that Eros includes other things besides sexual activity, I take for granted. . . . The carnal or animally sexual

element within Eros, I intend (following an old usage) to call Venus" (p. 85).

19. *Ibid.*, pp. 35, 37.

20. For further discussion of Christian charity in relation to *Nazarin*, see Gustavo Gutierrez, *A Theology of Liberation*, trans. and ed. by Sister Caridad Inda and John Eagleson (Maryknoll, New York: Orbis Books, 1973), pp. 199-200; and Peter Harcourt, *Six European Directors* (Baltimore: Penguin Books, 1974), pp. 122-23.

21. Freddy Buache, *The Cinema of Luis Bunuel*, trans. by Peter Graham (New York: A. S. Barnes & Co., 1973), p. 90.

22. *O Pagador de Promessas* (Keeper of Promises) is also the Brazilian title of the film.

23. Gene Phillips, S.J., in a study guide on *The Given Word* published by The National Center for Film Study (Box 772, Elmhurst, Ill. 60126).

24. *Images and Symbols* (New York: Sheed and Ward, 1969), p. 51.

25. *Homo Viator* (New York: Harper & Row, 1962), p. 130.

26. *Laurel British Drama: The Twentieth Century*, ed. Robert W. Corrigan (New York: Dell Publishing Co., Inc., 1965), p. 433.

27. For a sociological analysis of the film, cf. Eric Bergtal, "The Lonely Crowd in *La Dolce Vita*," *America* (October 7, 1961), 13-15.

28. Cf. Norman N. Holland, "The Follies Fellini," in *Renaissance of the Film*, ed. Julius Bellone (New York: The Macmillan Co., 1970), pp. 79-90.

29. "Playboy Interview: Stanley Kubrick," in *The Making of Kubrick's 2001*, ed. Jerome Agel (New York: New American Library, Inc., 1970), p. 328.

30. Of his musical composition Strauss has written: "I did not intend to write philosophical music or to portray in music Nietzsche's great work. I meant to convey by means of music an idea of the development of the human race from its origin, through the various phases of evolution, religious and scientific, up to Nietzsche's idea of superman." It is to be noted that the other idea explored by Nietzsche in *Zarathustra*—the idea of eternal recurrence—is not expressed in the music. Whether it is expressed in the film is open to question.

31. *Environmental Man* (New York: Harper & Row, 1969), p. 14. Interface is not unrelated to what Eisenstein meant by the juxtaposition of images in his concept of film form, or what Horace meant by a hot combination (*callida junctura*) of words in his *Ars Poetica*.

32. *Building the Earth* (Wilkes-Barre, Pa.: Dimension Books, 1965), p. 82.

33. Kubrick does not believe in God in a monotheistic sense. He imagines, however, that the universe must be filled with other intelligences, whose superiority may lead us to think of them as gods. Consistent with his inability to believe in God, he sees that "man has no crutch left on which to lean—and no hope, however irrational, to give purpose to his existence" (*The Making of Kubrick's 2001*, p. 352). As a consequence, man must create his own meaning. This last idea is also Nietzsche's.

34. This is the theme of Nathaniel Hawthorne's "My Kinsman, Major Molineux," discussed in Roy Harvey Pearce, "Hawthorne and the Sense of the Past, or, The Immortality of Major Molineux," *Journal of English Literary History* 21 (December 1954), 334.

35. *Filmguide to 2001: A Space Odyssey* (Bloomington, Ind.: Indiana University Press, 1973), p. 45.

36. *Ibid.*, p. 52.

37. *Ibid.*, p. 55.

38. Arthur C. Clarke, *2001: A Space Odyssey* (New York: New American Library, Inc., 1968), pp. 190-91.

Conclusion

THE ART OF FILM AS
SEARCH FOR MEANING

Our assumption throughout these analyses of films of quest has been that the discussion of meaning is best carried out in terms of the language of film itself. Certain cinematic techniques are more obviously related to the process of search and thus more regularly appropriated by directors in this genre. Thus aside from the question of visual imagery related to journey, we have discussed contemporary cinema's view of man's search for meaning in terms of composition of frame, of movement of the camera and movement within the frame, of types of visual continuity (i.e., narrative), and finally of editing.

Many theorists consider the choice and arrangement of physical reality to be the artistic essence of the film medium. For cinema of pilgrimage the road is that basic reality. However, while the designation of the dominant visual image sets the genre of film, it does not automatically tell us what the director's attitude toward quest is and therefore what we are to hope for man's future. It is only through an analysis of the director's treatment of physical reality (which in the fullest sense includes man of course) that we come to an understanding of his viewpoint.

The road is preeminently visible for example in *Easy Rider* and *The Last Picture Show*. Yet in the former it represents the illusion of freedom because of Billy's and Wyatt's lack of responsibility for the land; their violent deaths on the road mark the end of a bad trip. In the latter it suggests a successful passage into adulthood only for Sonny who remains in Anarene (close to the fleeting source of his inspiration); it is used by Duane and Jacy who have nowhere to go because they have nothing within to bring. Although the road is less prominent in *La Dolce Vita* and *The Passion of Anna*, it is nonetheless the implicit basis of the films' respective statements. Marcello and Andreas, as contemporary Everymen, descend into hell through the circles of their own need. The former seems to have lost all sense of direction; the latter, sensing two directions, is unable to choose either, and the road itself becomes an image of his cage.

Although Joe Buck in *Midnight Cowboy* is viewed finally against the background of the depersonalizing city, his journey nonetheless continues as the film ends and the movement itself bodes hope. Arlo is still on the move at the end of *Alice's Restaurant*; but his future, though obviously open-ended, lacks any substantive definition. *Scarecrow* begins on the road when Max and Lion are least free; it is simply another of Jerry Schatzberg's subtle ironies that at the end when Max is buying the bus ticket that supports his specific hope for himself and Lion the road is not seen but is very much present.

Vehicles often enough stress what we understand to be the film's statement about man's journey. The motorcycles in *Easy Rider* emphasize the dualism of its half-personalities; they are simply too "cool" to be genuine modes of passage. The bus that Joe Buck takes alone from Texas to New York and with Ratso to Miami carries in it the impersonalism of commercialized America. In *The Godfather* the waiting car goes nowhere; it brings death and leaves it. *Alice's Restaurant* varies the vehicle for each of its tentative contemporary approaches to the relationship between the individual and society.

In at least two of the films stairs replace the road as the focus of physical reality which viewed in relationship to man conveys the film's view of quest. In *The Rocking-horse Winner* stairs lead to the impasse of the attic room where Paul, responding compulsively to his mother's need, rides to his death on a hobby-horse. The steps leading up to the shrine of St. Barbara in *The Given Word*, on the other hand, carry Ze ultimately to the fulfillment of his vow, even if in death, as the doors of the church yield to the cross bearing his faithful body. *O Lucky Man!*, without ever appealing visually to stairs, makes ascent and descent the two sides of the same unhappy coin of chance accepted unreflectively.

The geographical or temporal direction of the journey often contributes a mythical dimension to man's quest. *Easy Rider* moves from West to East, reversing the pattern of American development; Billy and Wyatt, without having earned the right, are testing the nation's dream. An identical direction is traced in *Scarecrow* without, however, any of the same strong mythical overtones, simply the assurance that a return to origins can perhaps convert a selfish drifter into a selfless man. Although the initial West-to-East pattern of *Midnight Cowboy* emphasizes the humor of a Southwestern rude's onslaught on the Northeastern sexual establishment, it is the final journey from the cold North to the sunny South that supports the film's message of renewal through self-sacrifice. *Fellini Satyricon* uses this latter direction for its modest suggestion of Third-World hope. The mythical journey of Cal-Cain in *East of Eden* is superficially between the brooding coast (city) of his mother's sin and the sunlit valley (country) of Adam's righteousness, but only to adjust our vision to the coexistence of good and evil in each of us. In *Nazarin*, at least on the level of evangelical signals, it is the mythic journey of the savior from ministry in Galilee to conflict in Jerusalem.

Where the direction of the film journey depends upon the imaginative manipulation of time, irony seems almost invariably to be the reason. Isak Borg in *Wild Strawberries* returns to his past to discover the source of his present emptiness and unexpectedly finds some slender hope for his limited future. *Ballad of a Soldier* narrates the abortive history of a young hero's temporary leave to insist upon an irreversible threshold between youth and adulthood. The first part of *Ikiru* sketches the present despair of a terminal cancer patient, while the second reconstructs—through flashbacks—his discovery of ultimate meaning. *Slaughterhouse-Five* presents Billy Pilgrim's existence as "unstuck in time"; the bald statement that man is utterly incapable of altering the shape of life hides the intimation of a proposal for change. The deeper *2001: A Space Odyssey* probes the future of the universe the more surely Bowman's module resembles an infant in utero.

Frequently enough, as we have noted, the sea becomes an extension of the land and so of life's openness to meaning. The youths in *Fellini Satyricon* exhaust civilization's dreary potential; the promise of renewal must be supplied by the viewer of the film's final fragmented image of the sea. In Fellini's other apocalyptic work, *La Dolce Vita*, the young Umbrian angel who typifies life's promise of meaning is associated with the sea; and in a still earlier film of the same director, *La Strada*, the sea becomes Gelsomina the way "mourning becomes Electra."

And if the sea is an extension of land's journey, space is infinite-
ly so, even in *Slaughterhouse-Five* where it represents hope's
demand that we recall life's better moments as stimulus to renewal. *2001: A Space Odyssey* tempts us with unlimited possibility.

But physical reality as celebrated in film is aural as well as
visual. In *The Passion of Anna*, sheep bells, the clinking of cups
and saucers, and the ticking of a clock are sounds of silence that
emphasize man's estrangement. In a genre where time is of the
essence it is hardly surprising that measurements of time would
be conspicuous and significant. In *Wild Strawberries* a clock
without hands frightens Isak into thinking he has no time left.
In *Ikiru*, Mr. Watanabe, the bureaucrat, checks his watch constantly while his only consolation is the mere passage of time;
only after time has actually run out on Mr. Watanabe, the man
for others, do we see the girl's rabbit and his clock linked by his
mourners as symbols of ultimate meaning. Billy Pilgrim in
Slaughterhouse-Five is trapped by time just as he is by the clock
that pins him to the rubble of the once-glorious city where
Gothic clock towers had stood as proud reminders of former
meaning.

An aural accompaniment will sometimes be used to fortify
the quality of a man's passage. Gelsomina's poignant trumpet
call becomes a call to grace in *La Strada*; in *The Seventh Seal*
the cry of a lone bird announces the dance of death. The drums
at the end of *Nazarin* turn Nazario's painful steps into a con-
fident march. The exaggerated sound of David Bowman's
breathing in *2001: A Space Odyssey* intimates that man's passage into the future is through rebirth. And time after time in
our commentary we have noted the effective harmony or counterpoint of background music; with the exception of *O Lucky
Man!*, the chorus is heard but not seen.

Composition of frame, the basic component of film's visual
continuity, is of course highly instructive for discussions of
meaning. In *East of Eden*, until Adam accepts his son for what
he is as well as can be, Cal is shown at diagonal odds with reality. *The Last Picture Show* begins and ends with the movie
house dead center to the frame; it is a symbol of Anarene's
social bond, and its closing marks the death of a community

and an era. In *The Rocking-horse Winner* and *Alice's Restaurant*, there are frames within frames (windows, doors, arches, gates) and the import is similar: Paul and his mother are trapped by her greed for possessions; Arlo and his young friends are crowded out of the commune by the unresolved needs of Ray and Alice. Paul, unlike Arlo, is not old enough to recognize the trap in time. In *Scarecrow* and *Midnight Cowboy* the frame is even closer to the man—clothes. Max hides from the world in layers of protective clothing; Joe Buck tries unsuccessfully to deceive the world with his dated wrappings. The former signs his conversion by removing excessive layers, the latter by discarding his outfit altogether. Another kind of shroud, the coffin, reveals the limits of time to Isak Borg in *Wild Strawberries*, while Mr. Watanabe's spiritual death in *Ikiru* is seen in his interment by bureaucratic procedures. Recurring uterine enclosures in *2001: A Space Odyssey*—space station, capsules, suits, and the embryonic new man—remind us that man, the father of technology, is also its child; the film's final image arouses hope that he will break out of his self-confinement into the freedom of a new age.

Movement of the camera itself as well as movement within the frame lend themselves directly to the visual expression of quest. The promise of the closing shot of *Midnight Cowboy* is largely a factor of the continued movement of the bus into Miami carrying Joe Buck and the body of his friend Ratso, despite Joe's frightened look and the ominous reflection of the city's skyline in the window. And even though the narrative voice in *Fellini Satyricon* breaks off in midsentence and the movement of the ship out into the open expanse of inviting sea is interrupted, a sense of expectation nonetheless excites the viewer's imagination. The triumphal movement of the masses in *The Given Word* into St. Barbara bearing their sacrificial victim upon a cross conveys an assurance that even, or especially, through others one can fulfill a dream that was impossible alone.

Movement, however, can be abruptly frozen in the final sequence to emphasize loss of possibility as *Easy Rider* demonstrates so clearly. The sense of an ending is hardly less explicit in *The Last Picture Show* with a gradual pan of the camera;

however one projects Sonny's quest for meaning, the static centrality of the abandoned theatre in the film's final frame leaves no doubt about the passing of an era. Movement within the frame, moreover, cannot always be interpreted literally. In *Fellini Satyricon* where bodies and faces seem to be in perpetual motion, it is circular at best and without hope—prior to the final sequences. As Death leads the principal personages of *The Seventh Seal* across the hilltop in one of cinema's most compelling scenes, their dance is the "dance of death" and its movement celebrates ironically the triumph of limitation rather than the endurance of opportunity. Paul's frenetic last ride in *The Rocking-horse Winner* is another macabre dance of death; the excessive movement within the frame is frozen in place.

The angle of the camera, presupposing still another kind of movement, is often extreme enough in films of quest to shout the director's message. The almost vertical upward tilt of the camera in *Alice's Restaurant*, as light above the entrance to the Stockbridge church-commune is installed, and the miniscule wattage of the bulb tell us as much as any single image how remote their ideal of community is. Conversely, the downward tilt in *Ikiru* that makes the stairs Mr. Watanabe is climbing to his son seem like a hole stresses the rupture of their relationship and the impossibility of finding solace in a self-centered son. In both of Fellini's global judgments of contemporary society— *Fellini Satyricon* and *La Dolce Vita*—the camera tilts upward to note inaccessible levels of ascent: the massive Insula Felicles, shortly to be destroyed by earthquake, and the stairs leading to a suicide's apartment.

An episodic narrative structure seems most common in films of quest; it is a traditional feature of the genre of pilgrimage. One need think only of the prototypical *Pilgrim's Progress* to be satisfied on this count. Christian's flight from the City of Destruction and journey to the Celestial City past innumerable obstacles is straight linear ascent. Although this same episodic pattern endures into the genre of film odyssey, the progression is rarely progress pure and simple. Modern man's sense of hope or expectation from life infrequently touches the spiritual optimism of the Puritan classic. Only in *Scarecrow, La Strada, East of Eden*, and perhaps *The Given Word* do we sense uninterrupted linear development; the discovered meaning in each is analogous to traditional Christian anticipation. More often in current cinema the episodic structure suggests either life's frustrating sameness as in *O Lucky Man!* and *Slaughterhouse-Five* or man's continuing refusal to respond to life's challenge as in *Fellini Satyricon* and *La Dolce Vita*. The principal episodes of *2001: A Space Odyssey*, from the dawn of man to the future of exploration, remind us of life's enduring mystery as well as its repeated interface.

Editing is undoubtedly the single most effective and pervasive element of the process whereby the film experience eventually transmits to the viewer the excitement of quest itself. How can one discuss the development of imagery within a film (on which we have based so much of our commentary) unless it be from the impression created by the juxtaposition of images through editing? Expert editing alone is responsible, as we noted, for the success of Hill's visual adaptation of *Slaughterhouse-Five* over Vonnegut's novel. Coppola's brilliant indictment of man's hypocrisy is precisely stated in *The Godfather's* concluding sequence of intercut family christening and tribal vendetta. The almost subliminal flash-forward in *Easy Rider* showing Billy's and Wyatt's deaths is editing's way of telling us that their end was in their beginning. Without editing there is quite simply no finished work of art; and without analysis of film technique there can be no valid interpretation or genuine appreciation of film odyssey.

* * *

Our film odyssey has taken us down many roads and across many seas, even into the great expanse of space. We have seen ourselves at various stages and in many guises. A child begins his journey, as he must, seeking a sense of his own worth. He hopes to find it in a mother's love, but loses all his ventures if she is too preoccupied with her own self (*The Rocking-horse Winner*). He experiences a fall from innocence as he moves into a world where possibility is unlimited and love just another salable commodity (*O Lucky Man!*). But for good or evil a man has to choose. Even if he feels himself rejected, he must leave himself open to love (*East of Eden*). That love may indeed intimidate, until one discovers there is no answering the cry of the heart except in response to another (*Scarecrow*). A person's desire to love and be loved can be so all-consuming that one can reach even through death into the life of another human being (*La Strada*). The imminence of death can provoke a judgment upon the past and provide a meaning for the present, by moving one either to spend his remaining days in the service of others (*Ikiru*) or to open his heart to those for whose misery he is largely responsible (*Wild Strawberries*).

Very early in his journey a man is caught up in the desire for community as in the ebb and flow of a great sea. If, however, he attempts to create new forms of community without regard for the undercurrents of subconscious need, he will surely run aground (*Alice's Restaurant*). The passing of an era may plunge him in the vortex of a disintegrating society. At such a time, perhaps it is only the integrity of some other person that can save him (*The Last Picture Show*). But salvation is not owed to any man; there is no freedom without responsibility (*Easy Rider*). In the hope of salvation, one may venture into the city only to find damnation. The way out of this hell is through brotherly love and self-sacrifice (*Midnight Cowboy*). There is no turning back when the hell created by war snatches one from the relative security of one's youth and propels him into the fires of adulthood, effecting in brief time the passage from womb to grave (*Ballad of a Soldier*). It is possible to create one's own hell when the spiritual passage from death to life is deliberately contradicted by the forced passage from life to death in a world founded on fear and vengeance (*The Godfather*). Death and destruction face one at every turn, magnified to the point of absurdity by the technological expertise of modern warfare. If escape from reality cannot be the final answer, respect for the dignity of man may at least be a beginning (*Slaughterhouse-Five*).

Is there, then, at the very heart of reality, a deathless source of power and meaning? Is there a God to give ultimacy to man's search for meaning, to give to his journey a beginning *and* an end? The man who immerses himself in a world without

God becomes something less than man. There is no hope for him unless he pushes off to another shore (*Fellini Satyricon*). But if he allows himself to despair, his attempt to "pass over" is in vain; he can only move from rim to rim in the circle of his pain (*The Passion of Anna*). If God is calling, why can he not be heard? If he lives in light, why can he not be seen? Paradoxically, it is the man of simple faith who sees and hears (*The Seventh Seal*). Faith is inevitably shattered when one tries to enter the mystery of love without loving. A simple act of kindness may be enough to open the door again (*Nazarin*). When the act of faith expresses itself in a vow, a man dare not pause in his climb toward absolute reality for fear of losing himself on the way (*The Given Word*). When indeed he does pause and lets himself be tempted on every tier of his descent, shall he ever find his way up again (*La Dolce Vita*)? Only if he hears in the silence of his heart the call to pass beyond himself and, like Dante, makes himself ready for the stars (*2001: A Space Odyssey*).